SIMPSONS COMICS UNCHAINED

TITAN BOOKS

In loving memory of Snowball I:

We hope there are no shots, no vets, and no pet carriers in Kitty Heaven.

SIMPSONS COMICS UNCHAINED

Copyright ©1998, 1999, 2001 & 2013 by
Bongo Entertainment, Inc. All rights reserved.

Bongo Comics Group c/o Titan Books
1440 S. Sepulveda Blvd., 3rd Floor, Los Angeles, CA 90025

Published in the UK by Titan Books, a division of Titan Publishing Group,
144 Southwark St., London SE1 0UP, under licence from Bongo Entertainment, Inc.

FIRST EDITION: JANUARY 2002

ISBN 9781840234039

14 16 18 20 19 17 15

Publisher: MATT GROENING
Creative Director: BILL MORRISON
Managing Editor: TERRY DELEGEANE
Director of Operations: ROBERT ZAUGH
Art Director: NATHAN KANE
Production Manager: CHRISTOPHER UNGAR
Legal Guardian: SUSAN GRODE

Contributing Artists:
PETER ALEXANDER, KAREN BATES, TIM BAVINGTON, JEANNINE BLACK, SHAUN CASHMAN,
TIM HARKINS, CHIA-HSIEN JASON HO, NATHAN KANE, JAMES LLOYD, BILL MORRISON,
PHIL ORTIZ, JULIUS PREITE, MIKE ROTE, ERICK TRAN, CHRIS UNGAR

Contributing Writers:
IAN BOOTHBY, CHUCK DIXON, SCOTT M. GIMPLE, ROBERT L. GRAFF,
MATT GROENING, STEVE LUCHSINGER, TIM MAILE, JESSE LEON MCCANN,
BILL MORRISON, BILLY RUBENSTEIN, DOUG TUBER

PRINTED IN THE UNITED KINGDOM

TABLE OF CONTENTS

EL BARTO WAS H*

SORRY, BOYS, BUT YOU GRADUATED LAST SUMMER, AND AS THE DEAN, I HAVE TO GIVE YOUR DORM ROOM TO NEW, *PAYING* STUDENTS.

NOW IF YOU'LL EXCUSE ME, I'M LATE FOR THE *CHARLTON HESTON FILM FESTIVAL*. THE FIRST TWENTY HESTONS IN FULL COSTUME GET IN FOR *HALF PRICE!*

BUT... WHERE WILL WE *GO*? WHAT WILL WE *DO*?

COLLEGE WAS THE ONLY PLACE I *FIT IN*.

YOU MIGHT NOT BELIEVE THIS, BUT BACK IN HIGH SCHOOL I WAS A BIT OF A *GEEK*.

C'MON GUYS! IF *SPOCK* COULD COME BACK FROM THE DEAD, WE CAN DEAL WITH *THIS*.

YEAH, IF WE CAN FIND JOBS ON THE *GENESIS PLANET*.

HA!

HEE, HEE!

SNORT!

Y'KNOW, I THINK WE'RE GONNA BE *ALL RIGHT*.

LATER...

SPRINGFIELD NATURAL HISTORY MUSEUM

OKAY, THAT'S ENOUGH LEARNING. EITHER *BUY* SOMETHING AT THE GIFT SHOP OR *GET OUT!*

LATER, AT THE KWIK-E-MART...

HEY! THIS IS *NOT A LENDING LIBRARY!*

AND, AT THE LIBRARY...

HEY! THIS IS *NOT* THE *KWIK-E-MART!*

FINALLY, AT THE ANDROID'S DUNGEON COMIC BOOK EMPORIUM...

YES, YES, I AM WELL AWARE OF THE TREATY. ‹SIGH› YOU MAY STAY IN THE BACK ROOM FOR *ONE* NIGHT *ONLY.*

WE CLAIM *SANCTUARY* UNDER THE *SAN DIEGO COMIC CONVENTION CODE,* SUBSECTION...

YOU HAVE BEDS BACK HERE?

NO. YOU MAY SLEEP ON THE UNSOLD BOXES OF *SNOWBOARDING BATMAN* AND *PASSIVE-AGGRESSIVE WOLVERINE* ACTION FIGURES.

LATER...

Meet TV Star HENA Here Today!

ARE YOU SURE YOU DON'T WANT TO COME INSIDE, DAD? *HENA, DEMOCRATICALLY ELECTED PRINCESS,* REPRESENTS A FEMININE MERGING OF BOTH PHYSICAL STRENGTH AND EMOTIONAL INDEPENDENCE.

I'LL WAIT IN THE CAR, HONEY. DADDY WANTS TO LISTEN TO SPORTS ON THE RADIO.

AND NOW, HERE'S A CLIP FROM HENA'S *FIRST* APPEARANCE ON *TROY MCCLURE'S* FAILED SERIES, *THE ADVENTURES OF ACHILLES*.

HENA, COULD YOU GET THAT? MY FOOT'S *KILLING* ME!

WOW! A PLACE TO STAY *AND* WE GET TO MEET *HENA!* HER SERIES IS *FANTASTIC!*

EXCEPT FOR *EPISODE 37.*

C'MON, I THOUGHT *DON KNOTTS* MADE A *PRETTY GOOD* CENTAUR.

LOOK, IT'S *URKEL!*

NO... I'M NOT...

HE'S *DREAMY!*

GET HIM!

AND THE RED BALL FALLS IN. HE'S PULLING IT OUT. NOW HE'S SHOOTING THE PINK BALL. IT'S IN. NOW HE'S SHOOTING AT THE SAME RED BALL AGAIN...

AH, SNOOKER, MY SECRET SHAME.

BWAAAAH!

WHAT THE...

LOUSY BANK CALENDARS. THE CHEAP GLUE THEY USE NEVER LASTS PAST MARCH.

RACE YOU TO THE *TV*, DAD!

AWWWWW...*PBS*? THAT'S NOT ENTERTAINMENT; IT'S *ANTI*-TAINMENT.

THEY'RE DOING A 12-PART SERIES ON HOW WE CAN PROTECT THE ENVIRONMENT.

YOU'RE IN A GOOD MOOD. NOT STILL UPSET ABOUT *HENA*?

DAD, THAT WAS ALMOST A *WEEK* AGO.

WHEN CHAINING YOURSELF TO A TREE TO PREVENT LOGGING, THE KEY IS TO CHAIN YOURSELF TO THE *TRUNK*.

THE *TRUNK* IS THE KEY. REMEMBER, *THE TRUNK!*

THE *TRUNK*? OH, *DEAR GOD*, HOW COULD I *FORGET!*

NO, MR. SIMPSON. STAMPY IS FINE. HE'S STILL VERY HAPPY HERE AT THE GAME FARM. YES...HIS TRUNK IS FINE, TOO.

WELL, *THAT'S* A RELIEF!

HEY, HOMER, I WAS GETTING THE CROWBAR OUT OF THE TRUNK. DO YOU KNOW YOU'VE GOT THREE DEHYDRATED NERDS IN THERE?

EEYEW!

GLUB!

GASP!

LATER...

I DON'T WANT THEM LIVING IN OUR HOUSE. THEY'RE DISTURBING.

BUT, MARGE, THEY DON'T TAKE UP A LOT OF ROOM, AND THEY LIVE ON KRUSTY KREAMY-OS AND BUZZ COLA. THEY'RE LIKE *SEA MONKEYS* BUT WITHOUT THE *UPKEEP!*

OKAY, OKAY, THEY CAN LIVE HERE AS LONG AS THEY STAY IN THE GARAGE.

THANKS, MRS. SIMPSON.

YOU HAVE THE WISDOM OF *CAPTAIN SHERIDAN* AND THE BEAUTY OF *VAMPIRELLA.*

THE 1970'S *WARREN* VAMPIRELLA. NOT THE 90'S *SELL-OUT* VERSION.

UMM... THANK YOU.

DAY ONE.

KLAK! KLAK KLAK

DAY TWO.

KLAK! KLAK KLAK

DAY THREE

THEY'RE SO *BORING*. THEY DON'T *DO* ANYTHING. JUST LIKE THOSE *SEA MONKEYS*.

KLAK KLAK KLAK

YOU GONNA FLUSH 'EM TOO, HOMER?

SON, ONE DAY YOU'LL FIND OUT THAT NOT *ALL* OF OUR TROUBLES CAN BE FLUSHED DOWN THE *TOILET*.

FOR THE RECORD, NEITHER CAN GRAPEFRUIT.

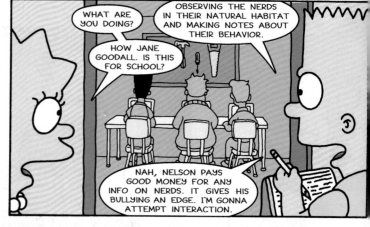

WHAT ARE YOU DOING?

OBSERVING THE NERDS IN THEIR NATURAL HABITAT AND MAKING NOTES ABOUT THEIR BEHAVIOR.

HOW JANE GOODALL. IS THIS FOR SCHOOL?

NAH, NELSON PAYS GOOD MONEY FOR ANY INFO ON NERDS. IT GIVES HIS BULLYING AN EDGE. I'M GONNA ATTEMPT INTERACTION.

IS THAT A VIDEO GAME?

YES, YOU HAVE TO SOLVE A SERIES OF INCREASINGLY DIFFICULT *NEW AGE* PUZZLES ON A *MYSTICAL* ISLAND.

WHERE'S THE VIOLENCE? IF THERE'S NO PARENT'S ADVISORY WARNING TO IGNORE THEN WHAT'S THE POINT?

WELL, WE *HAVE* BEEN WORKING ON SOMETHING A BIT EDGIER.

WHOA MAMA! BUT I CAN HARDLY SEE ANYTHING WITH ALL THIS *RAIN*.

THAT'S YOUR ENEMY'S *BLOOD*.

COOOOOL! HOW DO I GET A *BIGGER GUN*?

PASSWORD: *FREUD!*

OF COURSE THIS IS JUST A SMALL PART OF THE WHOLE GAME. WE NEED TO ADD THE ELVES, WIZARDS, ELABORATE CHARACTER CHARTS AND TONE DOWN THE VIOLENCE.

NEED BIGGER GUN!

KLAK KLAK

NOOOO! YOU JUST HIT THE *SEND* BUTTON. THE GAME WASN'T *FINISHED* YET!

NOW EVERYONE WITH A MODEM *HAS* IT! OUR REPUTATIONS AS PROGRAMMERS ARE *RUINED!*

WE'RE DEADER THAN AN *APPLE IIE*.

WELL, I SHOULD BE GOING...NOW... SEE YA.

THE NEXT MORNING...

I'M LATE FOR WORK. NO ONE BETTER BE SLEEPING UNDER THE CAR.

HEY...WHAT'S GOING ON? *KREAMY-OS* WITH *DOUBLE STUFF*? DID YOU GUYS BECOME MILLIONAIRES OVERNIGHT?

YEP! ORDERS ARE POURING IN FOR THE FULL VERSION OF OUR NEW GAME.

WE'RE RICHER THAN *DEAN HAGLUND!*

KLAK   KLAK   KLAK

VIDEO GAME, EH? Y'KNOW, BACK IN HIGH SCHOOL THEY USED TO CALL ME *MR. PONG!*

IT'S ABOUT A GUY WHO'S A *DEMONHUNTING*, UNDERCOVER, MILITARY BABE-MAGNET. WE CALL IT *DUMB* FOR SHORT.

WHY YOU LITTLE--!

REMINDS ME OF SOMEONE.

MR. SPARKLE?

THAT'S *IT!*

75% ARMOR

BULL 62 / 200
SHEL 26 / 50
ROKT 0 / 50
CELL 0 / 300

2 3 4 5 6 7

PAC MAN MOVE OVER, THERE'S A *NEW* GAME IN TOWN. WHAT THE EFFECT WILL BE ON *MS. PAC MAN* REMAINS TO BE SEEN.

BOYS, NOW THAT YOU'RE RICH, YOU REALLY SHOULD GET YOUR OWN PLACE.

WE'D LIKE TO MRS. SIMPSON, BUT WE HIRED AN INVESTMENT COUNSELOR. ALL OUR MONEY IS TIED UP IN LOW-RISK VENTURES.

LIONEL HUTZ, INVESTMENT ADVISOR AT YOUR *SERVICE!*

SORRY! SAY, YOU DON'T HAVE A *PAPER SHREDDER* AROUND HERE DO YOU?

GAAAH!

DON'T SNEAK UP ON PEOPLE LIKE THAT!

JUST RUB SOME CHEESE ON THEM AND GIVE 'EM TO THE DOG.

THANKS. NOW BOYS, I THINK IT'S IMPORTANT THAT YOU SEE WHERE YOUR MONEY'S *GOING.* DOUG, YOU'VE GOT A MEETING WITH...

TROY McCLURE, YOU MIGHT REMEMBER ME FROM SUCH FILMS AS...

I KNOW YOUR ENTIRE FILMOGRAPHY BY HEART MR. McCLURE: ALL THE PRESIDENT'S MONKEYS, ANDROID BEACH PARTY, BACK TO THE SEQUEL, BUTTER-THE MOTION PICTURE, THE COUGAR AND THE POLKA KING, CUT IT OUT-THE WACKY ADVENTURES OF JACK THE RIPPER, DRACULA'S DISCO-STUDIO FIFTY GORE, DRIVING MR. T...

SLOW DOWN! I'M *BLUSHING* ALREADY!

Y'KNOW, I REALLY SHOULD WRITE THAT DOWN SOME DAY, ALL THE....STUFF I DID.

YOU MEAN A RESUME?

BRILLIANT! RICH AND YOU SPEAK FRENCH...

HOW I ENVY YOU!

OH MY GOSH!

YOU KNOW WILLIAM SHATNER?

KNOW HIM? HE'S MY GARDENER!

YOU WEEDS SAY YOU WANT PEACE, YET YOU... ATTACK THESE INNOCENT TULIPS. WHEN WILL YOU LEARN? WHEN WILL WE...ALL...LEARN?

ARE YOU SURE YOU DON'T WANT A MINT JULEP?

ALCOHOLIC BEVERAGES GIVE ME EYE INFECTIONS, MR. MCCLURE.

DOUGLAS, I HAVE A DREAM! A DREAM TO MAKE THE GREATEST SCI-FI EPIC OF ALL TIME! YOUR MONEY CAN MAKE THAT DREAM COME TRUE.

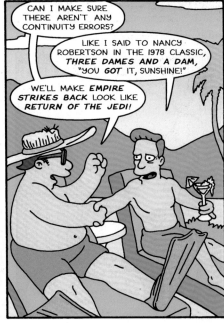

CAN I MAKE SURE THERE AREN'T ANY CONTINUITY ERRORS?

LIKE I SAID TO NANCY ROBERTSON IN THE 1978 CLASSIC, THREE DAMES AND A DAM, "YOU GOT IT, SUNSHINE!"

WE'LL MAKE EMPIRE STRIKES BACK LOOK LIKE RETURN OF THE JEDI!

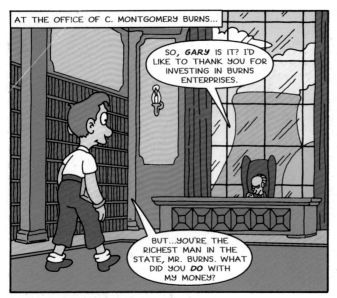

AT THE OFFICE OF C. MONTGOMERY BURNS...

SO, *GARY* IS IT? I'D LIKE TO THANK YOU FOR INVESTING IN BURNS ENTERPRISES.

BUT...YOU'RE THE RICHEST MAN IN THE STATE, MR. BURNS. WHAT DID YOU *DO* WITH MY MONEY?

SHWUK!

I THREW IT IN THE VAULT.

DEPTH GAUGE 80ft

$

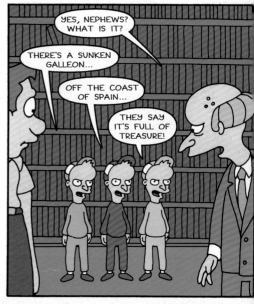

YES, NEPHEWS? WHAT IS IT?

THERE'S A SUNKEN GALLEON...

OFF THE COAST OF SPAIN...

THEY SAY IT'S FULL OF TREASURE!

I'M SORRY LADS. I'M BUSY WITH YOUNG GARY NOW. WE'LL HAVE THAT ADVENTURE ANOTHER TIME.

AWWWWWWWW!

19

DAD, YOU SHOULD BE PROUD! IT'S BEEN ALMOST *THREE WEEKS* SINCE THE NERDS LEFT THEIR COMPUTER COMPANY IN YOUR HANDS WHILE THEY CONTINUE TO WORK WITH TROY MCCLURE, PROFESSOR FRINK AND MR. BURNS, AND IT'S STILL A *THRIVING MULTI-MILLION DOLLAR BUSINESS.*

LISA, WHAT DID I TELL YOU ABOUT WORDY EXPOSITION AT THE DINNER TABLE?

RACE YOU TO THE TV, LISA?

AAAAAAAH!

TWANG!

HEH, HEH!

DAD, DO YOU EVER WORRY ABOUT *KARMA*?

HUH?

KARMA. REMEMBER, *SIDESHOW MEL* TALKED WITH *FIONA APPLE* ABOUT IT DURING KRUSTY'S SALUTE TO HINDUISM?

MMMMMMM... KARMA, MEL, APPLE!

ACTUALLY, BRINGING UP REINCARNATION WAS JUST A CHEAP WAY TO LEAD INTO A WEEK OF KRUSTY RERUNS.

HOMER, HERE'S THE LAST BEER IN THE HOUSE. WHOOOOOOOOOAH!

NOOOOOOOOOOOOOOO!

SOON...

SNIFF THAT POOR BEER.

LOUSY IRONIC RETRIBUTION.

WHAT I DON'T GET IS WHY THOSE NERDS LEFT *YOU* IN CHARGE OF THEIR COMPUTER COMPANY.

SOMETHING ABOUT GETTING A TAX WRITE-OFF FOR TAKING DANGEROUS RISKS.

ACTUALLY, I'VE NEVER REALLY *READ* THE TAX GUIDE, BUT THERE *COULD* BE SOMETHING LIKE THAT IN THERE.

WELL, TIME TO PASS OUT!

HEY, WHERE'S MOE?

I'M *MR. BLACK*. MOE CAN'T BE HERE THIS WEEK. HE'S ALL *TIED UP*... ON A VACATION...*DOWN UNDER*.

DRINK Duff BEER

LADIE'S NIGHT TUES

SO WHAT ELSE CAN I GET YOU GENTS?

MEANWHILE...

RETINA SCAN

IN THE LAST FEW WEEKS YOU'VE BECOME LIKE A *SON* TO ME, GARY.

VOICE REGISTER

TIME TO SHOW YOU HOW OUR ECONOMY *REALLY* WORKS.

TASTE TEST

YOU SEE, GARY, NO ONE *REALLY* UNDERSTANDS HOW THE ECONOMY WORKS, BUT NO ONE WILL *ADMIT* IT. ALL IT TAKES IS A FIRM HAND AND AN UNBLINKING STARE, AND THE WORLD IS YOUR OYSTER!

YOU HAVEN'T BLINKED YOUR EYES SINCE I MET YOU.

YES, BE A SPORT AND MOISTEN THEM, WOULD YOU?

ALL THAT ELUDES ME IS THE WORLD OF COMPUTERS. WITH YOUR EXPERTISE I CAN MASTER THE *COMMODORE 64* AND *CONQUER THE WORLD!*

SPRITZ!

HOMER, YOU SEEM LIKE AN INTELLIGENT MAN, SO I'M GOING TO LEVEL WITH YOU. I REPRESENT AN EASTERN COMPUTER SOFTWARE FIRM. WE'D LIKE TO BUY YOUR COMPANY.

WHAT'S YOUR COMPANY CALLED?

"VERY COMFORTABLE SASSY PANTS AND MODEMS YES." IT DOESN'T REALLY TRANSLATE WELL INTO ENGLISH.

SORRY, NOT INTERESTED! THOSE NERDS PUT THEIR *TRUST* IN ME!

WELL, I HAVE A *CONTRACT* HERE AND I'M PREPARED TO WAIT UNTIL YOU'RE DRUNK ENOUGH TO *SIGN* IT!

NOT GONNA HAPPEN. I ONLY HAVE *TEN BUCKS!*

CONTRACT

DID I MENTION ALL BEER TONIGHT IS *ON THE HOUSE?*

FOR EVERYBODY?

SURE. ANY FRIEND OF HOMER IS A FAMILY MEMBER OF OURS.

ACROSS TOWN, TROY MCCLURE'S SCI-FI EPIC IS ABOUT TO PREMIERE.

Free Screening: Troy McClure in *SATURNFORCE 3000*

I READ ON FILMGORIA'S WEB PAGE THAT THEY MADE THIS IN JUST *TWO WEEKS.*

I HEARD THEY SHOT THE FINAL SCENE *THIS MORNING.*

WHERE'S THE SOUND?

TURN IT UP!

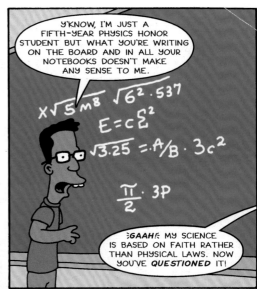

SO I GUESS WHAT I'M SAYING IS I'M SORRY I LET BARNEY SELL YOUR MULTI-MILLION DOLLAR COMPANY FOR PEANUTS.

I TOLD YOU--A BOWL OF PEANUTS.

HOW MUCH DID YOU GET?

AREN'T THOSE FREE IN BARS?

IT'S OKAY, MR. SIMPSON. "VERY COMFORTABLE SASSY PANTS AND MODEMS YES" HIRED US AS SOFTWARE DESIGNERS.

YEAH, WELL BARNEY ISN'T THE SAVVY BUSINESSMAN THAT *I* AM.

THEY LOST A LOT OF MONEY RECENTLY SO ALL THEY COULD GIVE US WAS ROOM AND BOARD. THEY *DID* FIND US THIS GREAT PLACE!

THE HIGH LIFE WASN'T FOR US. IT WAS LIKE WHEN *TASHA YAR* LEFT *NEXT GENERATION*, AND THEY MADE *WORF* HEAD OF SECURITY, AND *RIKER* GREW A *BEARD*.

IT WAS TOO MUCH, TOO FAST.

WE SIGNED A 75 YEAR CONTRACT. WE'LL BE TOGETHER IN THIS ROOM *FOREVER!*

BUT WE STILL HAVE A FEW MEMENTOS FROM OUR MILLIONAIRE DAYS.

KREAMY-OS WITH *TRIPLE* STUFF. SO THE LEGENDS WERE *TRUE!*

THE END

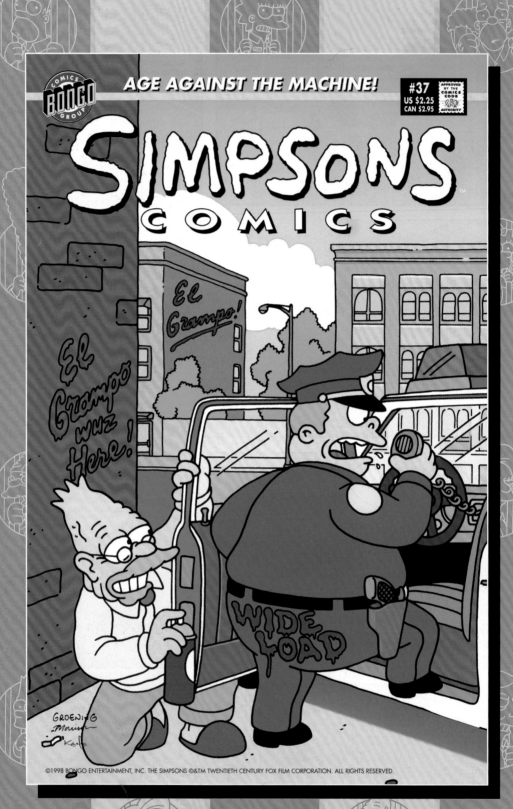

The Absent-Minded Protester

THIS IS REALLY *CREEPY*, MAN!

THE STENCH OF *DEATH* IS *EVERYWHERE*...

SCRIPT
DOUG TUBER
TIM MAILE
STEVE LUCHSINGER

PENCILS
PHIL ORTIZ

INKS
TIM BAVINGTON

LETTERS
JEANNINE BLACK

COLORS
NATHAN KANE

AMERICA'S MOST WANTED
MATT GROENING

A SURPRISE ATTACK HAS BEEN MADE ON OUR NAVAL BASE AT PEARL HARBOR! NOW, THIS IMPORTANT MESSAGE FROM OUR SPONSOR!

FOLKS, WHEN YOU'RE FEELING RUN DOWN, THERE'S NOTHING LIKE A DOSE OF *WESTPHAL'S AUXILIATOR* TO PEP YOU UP.

NEWS OF THE WAR CHANGED MY LIFE FOREVER!

THE HORRORS OF WAR SURROUNDED ME, BUT I WAS UNFLINCHING IN MY DUTY.

THOOM! THOOM!

I NEED THOSE POTATOES PEELED BY 1700 HOURS, SWABBO. I'M ENTERTAINING LATIN BOMBSHELL *LUPE VELEZ* FOR DINNER.

ADMIRAL "BULL" HALSEY HIMSELF SAID MY POTATOES O'BRIEN FIRED UP THE SPIRITS OF OUR FIGHTING MEN.

AS A GREAT WAR HERO, I HAD CLOUT. I EVEN ADDRESSED CONGRESS.

WHILE THE AUTOMOBILE IS A BOON TO OUR SOCIETY, I NONETHELESS RECOMMEND THAT, BEFORE 1950, WE ENACT *STRICT EMISSIONS CONTROLS* AND REQUIRE *AIR-BAGS* IN ALL MODELS. I ALSO THINK THE FRENCH INVOLVEMENT IN VIETNAM IS A CAN OF WORMS...

WELL, SIR, THAT IS YOUR PROBLEM RIGHT THERE. FOR ONE THING, NOBODY READS LETTERS ANYMORE. YOU'VE GOT TO GET *HIPPED-UP*, BY JOVE. PUT ON YOUR JAMS AND SURF...

KEEP OUT

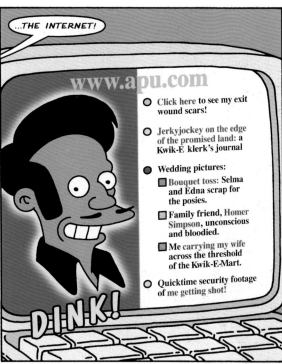

...THE INTERNET!

www.apu.com

○ **Click here** to see my exit wound scars!

○ Jerkyjockey on the edge of the promised land: a Kwik-E klerk's journal

● Wedding pictures:

☐ Bouquet toss: Selma and Edna scrap for the posies.

☐ Family friend, Homer Simpson, unconscious and bloodied.

☐ Me carrying my wife across the threshold of the Kwik-E-Mart.

○ Quicktime security footage of me getting shot!

DINK!

BUZZ COLA

www.apu.com

○ Click here to see my exit wound scars!

○ Jerkyjockey on the edge of the promised land: a kwik-e-klerk's journal

○ Wedding pictures:

INTERNET...BAH! I DON'T HAVE TIME FOR YOUR NEWFANGLED DOOHICKIES. I'M NOT GOING TO LISTEN TO ANY MORE OF YOUR CLAPTRAP!

BUT MAYBE APU'S RIGHT! MY WAYS ARE AS OLD-FASHIONED AS BEARDED PRESIDENTS.

JIMBO WAS HERE

SPRAYIN' THIS

Barto

33

AT THE SPRINGFIELD MALL...

WITHERED THOU GOEST
Clothing for the Feeble, Infirm and Decrepit Gentleman

I NEED A VERY SPECIAL OUTFIT...

Sale!

I DON'T LIKE ANY OF THESE. I'LL COME UP WITH SOMETHING ON MY OWN.

TUG! TUG!

YANK!

BEHOLD "EL GRAMPO!" LOOK UPON ME, OH WORLD, AND DESPAIR!

STANDING UP STRAIGHT IS A DAY'S WORK. I'D BETTER TAKE A NAP.

LATER THAT DAY...

NO MORE ENSLAVEMENT TO THE INDUSTRIAL LEVIATHAN! (AND BRING BACK WESTPHAL'S AUXILIATOR) "El Grampo"

SPRINGFIELD MILLS DISTRIBUTION PLANT

LORDY. SOME MYSTERIOUS PERSON HAS A POTENT MESSAGE TO GET OUT. I SAY AGAIN, LORDY.

AW, CRUD-- THEY'RE ONTO US.

KRUSTY KRUNCH KORN-FLAVORED TREETZ

END BASING OF PACKAGE WEIGHT BY VOLUME! "El Grampo"

IT TOOK ME A LONG TIME TO THINK UP ALL THOSE SWEAR WORDS, AND NOW THEY'RE SPRAYED OVER. THEY'RE GONE, MAN! ALL GONE!

WE LIVE BY THE RATTLING CAN, WE DIE BY THE RATTLING CAN. THERE, THERE.

STOP TAGGERS! "El Grampo"

EL GRAMPO STRIKES AGAIN!

I'M TERRIBLY COLD, AND NONE OF MY VITAL ORGANS DO WHAT THEY'RE SUPPOSED TO.

36

THE EL GRAMPO SPREE CONTINUES UNCHECKED, A MENACE TO SOCIETY WHICH RANKS WITH *JACK THE-RIPPER, AL CAPONE, THE UNABOMBER,* AND *SIMON BAR SINISTER,* WHO, WHILE A CARTOON CHARACTER, NEVERTHELESS CAUSED *UNDERDOG* THE SAME LEVEL OF GRIEF WE'RE ALL SUFFERING ON A DAILY BASIS.

QUIT MAKING SUCH AN INFERNAL RACKET! "*El Grampo*"

EXPERTS HAVE DETERMINED THIS IS NOT THE WORK OF YOUR GARDEN-VARIETY, DISENFRANCHISED, YOUTHFUL PUNK, BUT A CALCULATING, CLEVER DEMON IN HIS GOLDEN YEARS.

I CAN'T BELIEVE THIS WANNA-BE IS GETTING SUCH GREAT PRESS! HE'S *OBVIOUSLY* AN AMATEUR! LOOK AT HIS TAG! HE KICKED BACKSPRAY UP ALL OVER THE FUSELAGE. AND CHECK OUT THE *DRIPPAGE*... AND THE LACK OF *RIBALDRY!*

I DON'T WISH TO SOUND INFLAMMATORY OR GO OFF HALF-COCKED, BUT THE OBVIOUS SOLUTION IS TO ROUND UP EVERYONE OVER THE AGE OF SEVENTY AND HAVE THEM PUT SWIFTLY TO DEATH!

HMMMM... I DON'T APPROVE OF A PERSON BECOMING A CELEBRITY BY DEFACING PROPERTY--I DON'T REALLY APPROVE OF CELEBRITIES, PERIOD--BUT I THINK THAT SOLUTION IS A BIT HARSH.

OH C'MON, MARGE. PUTTING HIM TO DEATH WOULD BE *GOOD* FOR HIM. IT WOULD GIVE HIM INCENTIVE.

GERIATRIC FREAK TERRORIZES CITY... WAIT'LL THEY GET A LOAD OF *ME*...

LET'S GO *LIVE* TO *SPRINGFIELD ELEMENTARY* FOR THE WIGGUM PRESS CONFERENCE, ALREADY IN PROGRESS.

WITH THE *SPRINGFIELD 500* COMING UP, I JUST WANT TO SERVE NOTICE TO THIS SO-CALLED "*EL GRAMPO,*" THAT WE *WILL NOT* HAVE GRAFFITI MARRING OUR BELOVED EVENT.

AND BECAUSE THE LAW-ENFORCEMENT COMMUNITY OF SPRINGFIELD IS *COMPLETELY POWERLESS* TO STOP HIM, WE'RE TAKING STEPS TO CLEAN UP THE TAGGING. THE FOLLOWING PARKING VIOLATION OFFENDERS ARE HEREBY PLACED ON GRAFFITI-REMOVAL DETAIL. IN ALPHABETICAL ORDER, *SAMPSON, HOMER,* AND *SIMPSON, HOMER.*

D'OH!

CORRECTION, THAT WAS A TYPO. THE TWO ON GRAFFITI-REMOVAL WILL BE *SIMPSON,* HOMER, AND SIMPSON, HOMER.

D'OH! D'OH!

THAT'S IT! EL GRAMPO IS AN EL *HACKO!* I'M ROOTIN' THIS COOT OUT!

HOW?

ELEMENTARY, MY DEAR LISA. *SPRINGFIELD ELEMENTARY!*

BART'S BIG BOOK OF VANDALISM

SOON...

BULL'S-EYE!

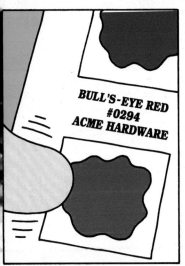

BULL'S-EYE RED
#0294
ACME HARDWARE

LATER...

$9.99

WHAT THE--?? GEEZ, GRAMPA. LEAVE SOME FOR EL GRAMPO!

THINGA-MAJIGS! $2.69 lb

I NEED TEN CANS OF NEWCASTLE BLUE, AND TEN CANS OF BULL'S-EYE RED.

OH, BOY. OH, GOSH.

EL GRAMPO ALERT

FALSE ALARM

CALLING ALL CARS! WE HAVE AN ALARM AT 1563 ROSEMONT WAY. FOOTSPEED FOR AN AVERAGE MAN IS FIVE MILES PER HOUR. YOUR FUGITIVE'S NAME IS *EL GRAMPO!*

HE GAVE US THE SLIP FELLAS. HE'S A FIEND SENT FROM THE BOWELS OF PERDITION.

GETTIN' DARK. TIME TO DO THE SWITCH-A-ROO!

COULD YOU GIVE MY BROGAN A TUG, MA'AM?

NOT EVEN IF YOU WERE THE LAST SINGLE MAN ON EARTH, METHUSELAH.

LATER...

AND I MEAN IT! EL GR

EL GRAMPO, I PRESUME...

AGGHH! WHO'S THAT? I NEARLY SWALLOWED MY TEETH.

GRAMPA?! IS THAT *YOU*?

I STILL DON'T BELIEVE IT. Y... YOU KILLED THAT EL GRAMPO GUY AND STOLE HIS CLOTHES. RIGHT?

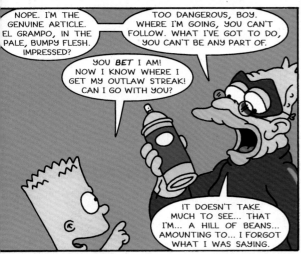

NOPE. I'M THE GENUINE ARTICLE. EL GRAMPO, IN THE PALE, BUMPY FLESH. IMPRESSED?

TOO DANGEROUS, BOY. WHERE I'M GOING, YOU CAN'T FOLLOW. WHAT I'VE GOT TO DO, YOU CAN'T BE ANY PART OF.

YOU *BET* I AM! NOW I KNOW WHERE I GET MY OUTLAW STREAK! CAN I GO WITH YOU?

IT DOESN'T TAKE MUCH TO SEE... THAT I'M... A HILL OF BEANS... AMOUNTING TO... I FORGOT WHAT I WAS SAYING.

BUT GRAMPA, I WANT TO GO WITH YOU, TO HELP YOU FACE THE DANGER. I LOVE YOU GRAMPA... AND IF YOU DON'T TAKE ME, I'LL RAT YOU OUT BEFORE YOU EVEN KNOW WHAT HIT YOU.

HE THREATENED TO HAVE ME PROSECUTED TO THE FULL EXTENT OF THE LAW! WHY, THAT MUST MEAN... HE RESPECTS ME!

RIGHTY-O, THEN. LET'S ROLL.

AND SO IS BORN THE MOST PROLIFIC PARTNERSHIP IN TAGGING HISTORY-- *EL BARTO AND EL GRAMPO!*

EL GRAMPO AND EL BARTO RULE!

EL GRAMPO AND EL BARTO RULE!

EL GRAMPO AND EL BARTO RULE!!

3407

EL GRAMPO

MPO RU

HEY EVERYBODY, MEET MY GRANDSON. HE'S VISITING ME, AND HE DOESN'T EVEN *HAVE* TO!

SURE, SIMPSON--THINK YOU'RE *COCK-OF-THE-WALK* BECAUSE YOU HAVE A RELATIVE WHO ISN'T PRETENDING YOU'RE DEAD. WELL, JUST WAIT TILL MY BIRTHDAY WHEN MY SON'S REALTOR SENDS ME A CALENDAR. *YOU'LL* WHISTLE A DIFFERENT TUNE.

HEY GRAMPA, TELL ME AGAIN HOW YOU TAGGED *MAYOR QUIMBY'S* HOUSE.

WASN'T QUIMBY'S HOUSE, IT WAS *QUIMBY*. YOU'RE KINDA INTERESTED IN MY STORIES NOW, EH, BOY?

THEY'RE WAY BETTER NOW. BEFORE, YOUR MOST EXCITING STORY WAS ABOUT WAVING AT SOME GUY NAMED *ADLAI STEVENSON* DURING A PARADE.

EL GRAMPO REMAINS AT LARGE, SO I'M INSTITUTING A CITY-WIDE DRAGNET TO APPREHEND THIS FUGITIVE.

I WANT A HARD-TARGET SEARCH OF EVERY *DOGHOUSE, HENHOUSE, GREENHOUSE* AND *OUT-HOUSE* IN SPRINGFIELD. I PERSONALLY WILL COVER EVERY *STEAKHOUSE* AND *HOUSE OF PANCAKES*, AND ANY OTHER DINER WITH A HOMEY ATMOSPHERE, OR WHERE THE MENU PUNCHES OUT INTO A *PIRATE MASK*.

WIGGUM! THAT GUY COULDN'T APPREHEND A *DEAD TURTLE!*

LOOKS LIKE THE FUZZ IS COMING DOWN ON US. WELL, I GUESS OUR REIGN OF TERROR IS OVER. I'LL JUST GO BACK TO THE *ADLAI STEVENSON* STORY. HE WAS RIDING IN A '49 *DESOTO*. WAVED RIGHT AT ME, BIG AS DAY.

BUT GRAMPA, YOU HAVEN'T GOT YOUR *WESTPHAL'S AUXILIATOR* YET! I SAY WE TAKE ONE MORE SHOT AND GO OUT IN A *BLAZE* OF SELF-DESTRUCTIVE *GLORY!*

BUT IT'S TOO *DANGEROUS* OUT THERE. I COULD GET *CAUGHT* AND SPEND THE REST OF MY LIFE IN *SUPERVISED CONFINEMENT*.

"BRING BACK WESTPHAL'S AUXILIATOR." WHY, *I* REMEMBER THAT PRODUCT! IT ALWAYS PUT A LITTLE ZIP IN MY GET-ALONG, WHEN I WAS FEELING POORLY.

THAT'S WHAT YOU'VE GOT MY SPECIAL "*KICKAPOO JOY JUICE*" FOR, SIR.

I WANT THE *AUXILIATOR!* I KNOW! I'LL BUY THE COMPANY THAT USED TO MANUFACTURE IT AND RESUME PRODUCTION, *TOOT-SWEET!*

THERE'S THE SCOFFLAW, BOYS. *SHOOT TO KILL!*

BUT I DON'T WANT TO GET IN TROUBLE WITH DUFF'S LAWYERS, SO TRY NOT TO HIT THE... AW, *NERTS!*

KA-CHOW!

SSSSSSSS

WHOA, NELLY!

AAAAAIIIIYEEEEEE!

FWOOF!

D'OH! THE HUMANITY!

IF WE GET OUT OF *THIS* ONE ALIVE, YOU'LL HAVE A *GREAT* STORY TO TELL.

AND IF WE *DON'T*, WHEN THE COPS FIND OUR CHARRED, TWISTED SKELETONS, IT'LL GIVE 'EM NIGHTMARES, SO THE JOKE'LL BE ON *THEM*.

AIN'T NO FOUNTAIN DRY ENOUGH

CONVENIENT

DELIVERY AND INSTALLATION

SPRINGFIELD RETIREMENT CASTLE

SSSSSSSS

SPLOOOSH!

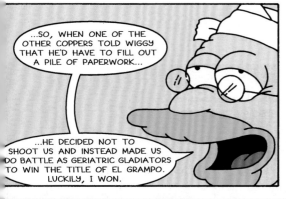

...SO, WHEN ONE OF THE OTHER COPPERS TOLD WIGGY THAT HE'D HAVE TO FILL OUT A PILE OF PAPERWORK...

...HE DECIDED NOT TO SHOOT US AND INSTEAD MADE US DO BATTLE AS GERIATRIC GLADIATORS TO WIN THE TITLE OF EL GRAMPO. LUCKILY, I WON.

SO THAT'S THE STORY OF HOW YOUR GRAMPA BECAME A CARBUNKLE ON SOCIETY'S KIESTER! I CHANCED *DEATH!* I *LAUGHED* IN THE FACE OF *JOHN LAW!* I STAYED AWAKE *LOOOOONG* PAST MY BEDTIME!

GLUG! GLUG!

ALL OF IT, JUST TO STAND UP, BE COUNTED, AND STOP BEING IGNORED! IT WAS ALL WORTH--

PRUNE JUICE

PRUNE JUICE

LARGE TEXT MAGAZINE

BUH-DAH-BUP-TAH!

HERE, GRAMPA.

WESTPHAL'S AUXILIATOR! WHERE IN THE NAME OF WILFORD BRIMLEY--

THE KWIK-E MART JUST STARTED STOCKING IT. I FOUND IT IN THE POWDERED ITEMS SECTION WHERE DAD HANGS OUT.

THANKS, BOY. YOU KNOW, ALL THIS REMINDS ME OF WESTPHAL'S OLD SLOGAN. "IT DOESN'T MATTER IF YOU GET OLD AND ARE SUBSEQUENTLY IGNORED BY FRIENDS, LOVED ONES, AND THE GENERAL PUBLIC, YOU CAN STILL HAVE PEP WITH WESTPHAL'S!"

WELL, ENJOY.

OH, I WILL. BELIEVE ME, I *WILL!*

WHAT DID YOU GET ME AGAIN?

THE END

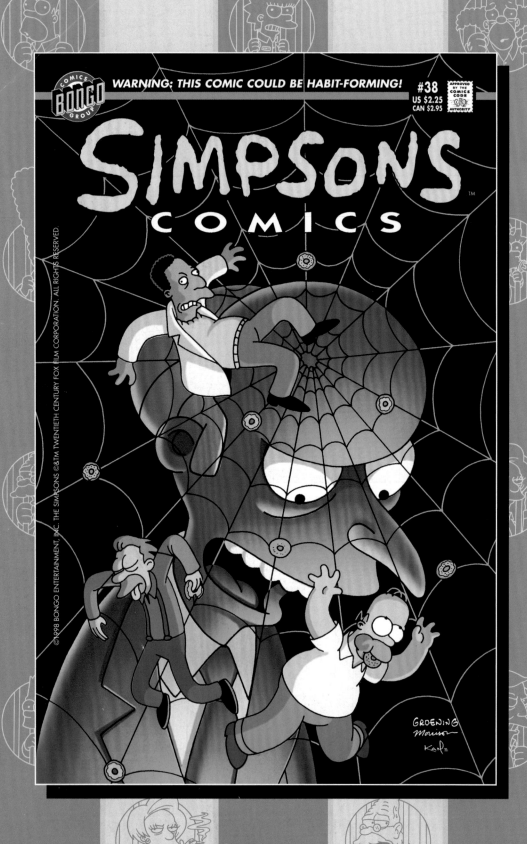

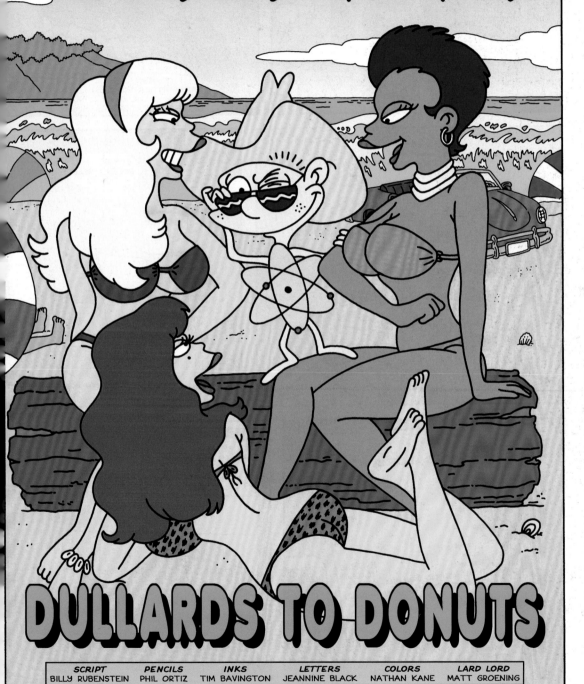

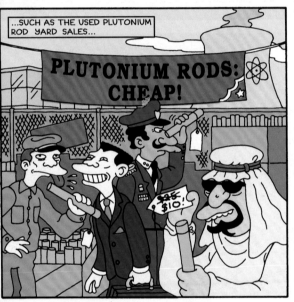

KEEP UP THE FINE WORK OLBERMAN.

DRAT, WE'RE NOT MOVING. OH, FIDDLESTICKS. THIS HAPPENS SOMETIMES.

OLBERMAN, SEE TO IT THAT MY INTER-OFFICE TRANSPORTATION SYSTEM IS REPAIRED FORTHWITH.

UH, YES SIR.

VRRRR RRRRR!

?

I JUST DESPISE INEFFICIENCY.

AND NOW, SMITHERS, THE NEXT STEP IN MY PLAN.

AHOY, HOY. THIS IS MR. BURNS...

...I AM AFRAID THAT, DUE TO BUDGETARY CONCERNS, I WILL BE UNABLE TO FURTHER PROVIDE YOU WITH YOUR DAILY SUPPLY OF DONUTS. THAT IS ALL. CARRY ON.

60

I DON'T WANT TO BE A GRIPERINSKI, BUT BUSINESS AT THE LEFTORIUM *HAS* BEEN DOWN MIGHTILY-ITILY AS OF LATE. I PROMISED ROD AND TODD I'D TAKE THEM TO SEE THE "RELIGIOUS OVERTONES JAZZ BAND", BUT I DON'T KNOW IF I'LL BE ABLE TO *AFFORD* IT.

HMMM.

LEFT HANDERS RULE!

I ♥ SOUTH PAWS

POSTERS

KISS ME I'M LEFT HANDED

SALE

BARGAIN BOX

AND BECAUSE THE PRIMARY WAGE PROVIDERS OF THIS COMMUNITY NO LONGER BESTOW THEIR LARGESS ON THEIR LITTLE RUGRATS, I HAVE AN UNWANTED SURPLUS OF RADIOACTIVE MAN AND SUPERIOR SQUAD PARAPHERNALIA. BECAUSE OF MY FINANCIAL STRAITS, I WILL NOT BE ABLE TO ATTEND THIS YEAR'S TRIBUTE TO THE UNDER APPRECIATED SCI-FI WORK OF THE GREAT RICARDO MONTALBAN AT THE "CANNES KHAN CON."

HMMM.

ITCHY

YES, MARGE, OUR COFFERS ARE RUNNING QUITE DRY AT THE MOMENT. I WAS HOPING TO ADD A STROBE LIGHT AND DOLBY SOUND SYSTEM TO OUR NATIVITY SCENE THIS YEAR, BUT AT THIS RATE, WE'LL BE LUCKY IF WE CAN AFFORD *TWO* WISE MEN.

HMMM.

Raspberry Sparkling Holy Water

Where's Waldo In The Bible

MOSES TRANS MONTHLY

YOU WANT A SPECIAL TOWN HALL MEETING TO...AH... DETERMINE IF THE DONUTS AT THE POWER PLANT POSE...AHEM...A SERIOUS HEALTH THREAT? YOU *GOT* IT. SALES AND INCOME TAXES ARE SO FAR DOWN, I'VE HAD TO CANCEL THREE...EH...JUNKETS AND FOUR TRYSTS. I DON'T CARE HOW MUCH BURNS IS BRIBING ME...AHEM...I MEAN HOW MUCH MONEY MR. BURNS HAS, THE FINANCES OF SPRINGFIELD'S PROSTITU...ER...I MEAN POPULACE, COMES FIRST!

MAYOR QUIMBY

MEANWHILE...

SMITHERS, WHAT'S THE MEANING OF THIS? WHY ARE THERE PEOPLE PROTESTING OUTSIDE MY PLANT?

NUCLEAR POWER IS DA BOMB!

SMILIN' JOE, YOU'RE SO SEXY!

Get that Sinful, Sinkin' Feeling!

STOP TARGETING OUR KIDS

DUNK THIS!

Sinful Sinkers: The Real Devil's Food Cake

What's in those things anyway?

What's the deal with the hole?

GABBO RULES!

WELL SIR, IT APPEARS THAT YOU'VE BEEN CALLED TO APPEAR BEFORE A SPECIAL TOWN HEALTH COMMISSION, FOR "DISTRIBUTING AN ADDICTIVE SUBSTANCE WITHOUT A WARNING AND ATTRACTING CHILDREN TO AN ADDICTIVE SUBSTANCE THROUGH DEMOGRAPHICALLY TARGETED ADVERTISING." THEY WANT TO DISCUSS THE DONUTS, SIR.

WHAT A COINCIDENCE...

...THAT IS *EXACTLY* WHAT *I* WOULD LIKE TO DISCUSS AS WELL.

WHO ARE YOU? WHAT DO YOU WANT?

LET'S JUST SAY THAT I AM A "LEGITIMATE BUSINESSMAN" WITH A BUSINESS PROPOSITION HAVING TO DO WITH A MUTUAL BUSINESS INTEREST IN THE WORLD OF BUSINESS. DO YOU GET MY DRIFT?

Smithers   Security   Dancing Bears

SO WHAT YOU'RE SAYING IS THAT IF I CUT YOU IN ON THE ACTION, YOU'LL HELP ME WITH MY LITTLE TOWN MEETING, YOU WON'T CAUSE TROUBLE AT MY PLANT, YOU WON'T CAUSE ANY WORK SLOWDOWNS, SHUTDOWNS, OR MELTDOWNS, AND YOU'LL BE SO KIND AS TO NOT BREAK ANY OF MY APPENDAGES. IS THAT THE *GIST* OF YOUR *DRIFT*?

PRECISELY.

SPLENDID. THEN WE HAVE A DEAL. SMITHERS WILL GIVE YOU A STANDARD EXTORTION CONTRACT ON YOUR WAY OUT.

AND SMITHERS, SUMMON THE LAWYERS, SCIENTISTS, AND SHILLS OF *D.U.P.E.D.*

WHEW, I'M HERE... ⸂GASP⸃...MR. BURNS, I... ⸂WHEEZE⸃...CAME AS FAST AS I...⸂HUFF⸃...COULD. OH BOY...⸂WHEW⸃.

AND ONCE UPON A TIME, IN A ROOM MUCH LIKE THIS ONE, YOUR WASTREL PRESENCE WAS *REQUIRED*, BUT THAT MOMENT HAS LONG SINCE PASSED. SEE THESE FINE TOUGHS TO THE EXIT. GOOD DAY.

I'M *KENT BROCKMAN* FOR *"SMARTLINE"*. TONIGHT, *SMILIN' JOE'S SINFUL SINKERS*. A TASTY PASTRY THAT'S NUTRITIOUS AND GOOD FOR THE WHOLE FAMILY, OR A PRODUCT WRONGFULLY ACCUSED BY A BUNCH OF OVERZEALOUS SAFETY FREAKS WITH TOO MUCH TIME ON THEIR HANDS?

WE'LL BE BACK WITH THIS REPORT RIGHT AFTER THIS MESSAGE FROM OUR NEW SPONSOR, *SMILIN' JOE'S SINFUL SINKERS*.

CITY HALL

TONIGHT: SPECIAL HEALTH COMMISSION EXAMINES DONUTS.

TOMORROW: SPECIAL VIDEO COMMISSION EXAMINES PORN (BYO PORN & DONUTS).

AHEM. I CALL THIS... EH...SPECIAL HEARING TO ORDER. MR. BURNS, WOULD YOU PLEASE RISE?

DO YOU...EH...SWEAR TO TELL THE TRUTH, THE WHOLE TRUTH, AND NOTHING BUT THE...EH...TRUTH?

I DO.

I AM JUST AN OLD, SIMPLE MAN. I KNOW VERY LITTLE ABOUT GORMANDIZING HABITS, NUTRITIONAL SCIENCE, OR ANY OF THESE OTHER COMPLICATED MATTERS. I MERELY WANT TO GIVE MY WELL-DESERVING WORKERS A LITTLE EXTRA SOMETHING BACK IN EXCHANGE FOR ALL OF THEIR SWEAT AND TOIL.

THEY SEEM TO LIKE THESE ROUND, PASTRY TREATS WITH THE WHIMSICAL HOLE IN THE MIDDLE, SO THAT'S WHAT I GIVE THEM.

MMM...WHIMSICAL HOLE.

NOW AS FOR THE SCIENCE OF THE MATTER, I GIVE YOU MY ESTEEMED COLLEAGUE, DR. OLBERMAN, FROM THE DONUT UNION PUBLIC EDUCATION DIVISION.

I KNOW HOW DRY AND INTIMIDATING COMPLICATED SCIENTIFIC MATTERS CAN BE TO THE LAYPERSON, SO I'M GOING TO TRY AND KEEP IT SIMPLE.

MEMORY   HAPPINESS   HUNGER

WOO-HOO!   ALL RIGHT!   SIMPLIFY!

MEMORY   HAPPINESS   HUNGER

DONUTS ARE NOT ONLY *NOT* HARMFUL, THEY ACTUALLY PROVIDE MANY NEUROLOGICAL BENEFITS, SUCH AS REDUCING STRESS, IMPROVING MEMORY, AND DECREASING APPETITES. IN FACT, EVERY TEST WE'VE CONDUCTED CONCLUSIVELY PROVES THAT AFTER CONSUMING DONUTS, THE SUBJECTS ARE LESS HUNGRY, THEY ARE HAPPIER, AND THEY CAN REMEMBER *WHY* THEY ARE HAPPY.

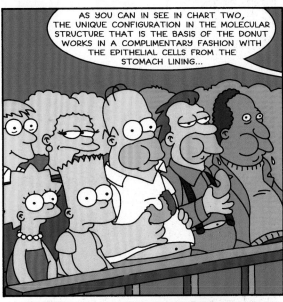

AS YOU CAN IN SEE IN CHART TWO, THE UNIQUE CONFIGURATION IN THE MOLECULAR STRUCTURE THAT IS THE BASIS OF THE DONUT WORKS IN A COMPLIMENTARY FASHION WITH THE EPITHELIAL CELLS FROM THE STOMACH LINING...

...AND CHART SEVENTY-SIX CLEARLY DEMONSTRATES HOW EACH DONUT HAS A UNIQUE DNA BLUEPRINT WHICH PROVIDES THE YUMMY FLAVOR THAT YOU ENJOY SO MUCH. SO, IN CONCLUSION, AS A MEMBER OF THE NON-BIASED, IMPARTIAL SCIENTIFIC COMMUNITY, I BELIEVE THAT NOT ONLY ARE THESE DONUTS NOT HARMFUL, THEY ARE ACTUALLY QUITE BENEFICIAL TO THOSE WHO CONSUME THEM. THANK YOU.

ZZZZZZZZZZZZZZZZZZZZZZZ

EVERYBODY WAKE UP! HE'S FINISHED!

MEMORY   HAPPINESS   HUN

I...EH...WOULD LIKE TO THANK *BIRCH BARLOW* FOR HIS...AHEM... REMARKS AND WOULD LIKE TO REMIND ALL OF HIS LOYAL FANS WHO VOTE FOR WHOEVER HE TELLS THEM TO THAT I...AHEM... CONSIDER *MYSELF* AN *"ECHO-DRONE"*. NOW, IS THERE...EH... ANYONE ELSE WHO WOULD LIKE TO SPEAK?

I HAVE SOMETHING I'D LIKE TO SAY.

THE CHAIR RECOGNIZES THE WOMAN WITH THE...EH... UNIQUE HAIRDO.

MY NAME IS MARGE SIMPSON, AND I DON'T HAVE ANY SCIENTISTS OR FAMOUS PERSONALITIES TO BACK ME UP...

...BUT I KNOW THAT AS A WIFE, A MOTHER, AND A CONCERNED MEMBER OF THIS COMMUNITY THAT I'M WORRIED ABOUT THE EFFECTS THAT THESE DONUTS ARE HAVING.

THEY HAVE NO NUTRITIONAL VALUE, THEY'RE BANKRUPTING EVERYONE EXCEPT MR. BURNS, THE ADVERTISEMENTS ARE AIMED AT CHILDREN, AND ALTHOUGH I CAN'T PROVE IT, I'D SWEAR THAT THEY'RE *ADDICTIVE*.

SHE HAS A POINT.

I HADN'T THOUGHT OF THAT.

THAT'S TRUE.

I'M THE OWNER OF *LARD LAD DONUTS,* AND NO ONE IS TAKING *MY* BUSINESS WITHOUT A *FIGHT!* I HAD ONE OF THESE SMILIN' JOE'S SINFUL SINKERS EXAMINED...

...AND WHAT I FOUND IN THEM WAS *SHOCKING!* WHAT I FOUND WAS...

NOW!

PARDON ME.

COMING THROUGH!

BAM!

WHAT'S GOING ON?!

WARNING!

It is believed by some that consuming these donuts in great quantities constitutes a health risk. We think those people are morons. You're not a moron, are you?

WEEKS LATER...

HMMM. *THIS* DOESN'T LOOK GOOD.

EXPENDITURES ON DONUTS

WORKER PRODUCTIVITY

SMITHERS, WHAT IS THE *MEANING* OF THIS? I'M GIVING THESE WORKERS ALL THE DONUTS THEY WANT. WHY ARE THEY NOW *LESS* EFFICIENT?

SIR, I THINK THE ANSWER IS ON THE MONITORS.

DANGER!

WARNING

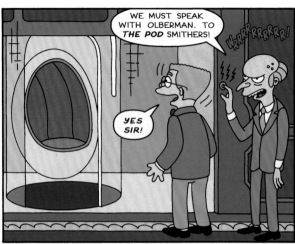

THE END

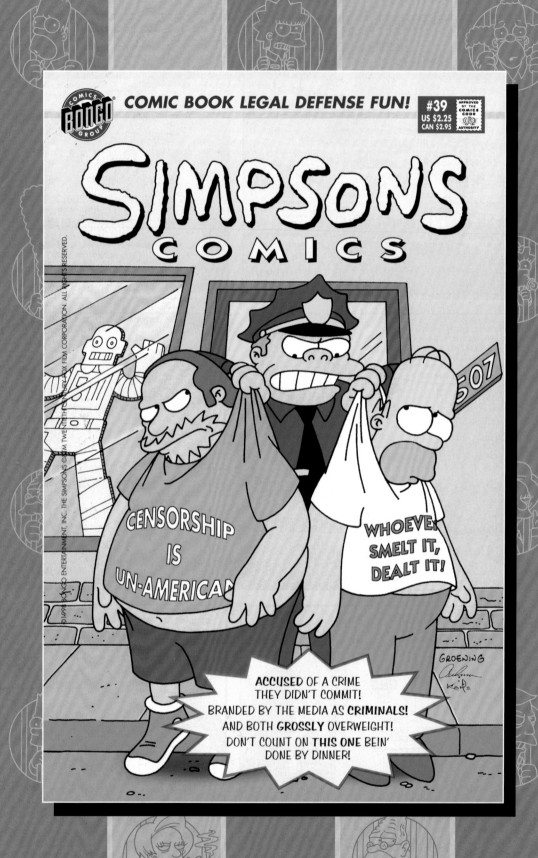

BENJAMIN FRANKLIN:
BIG BAD MUTHA OF INVENTION

...AND THAT'S HOW BENJAMIN FRANKLIN INVENTED ELECTRICITY. HE WENT ON TO INVENT OTHER USEFUL STUFF LIKE THE *ODOMETER* AND *FRANCE*. HE ALSO--

BART.

YOU'RE NOT BUYIN' ANY OF THIS, ARE YOU?

I STOPPED LISTENING WHEN YOU CALLED HIM *THE BENJSTER.*

SOON...

DID YOU *REALLY* THINK YOU'D GET AWAY WITH IT, BART? THANKS TO *YOU,* YOUR CLASS NOW THINKS THAT *BENJAMIN FRANKLIN* WAS A VENGEFUL, TREE-HATING, GIANT-BELT-BUCKLE-WEARING, KITE-WIELDING *MANIAC!* AND MY CONTACTS TELL ME THAT YOU'RE SPREADING A RUMOR THAT *DAVY CROCKETT* WORE A JAUNTILY-ASKEW *BOWLER* INSTEAD OF A *COONSKIN CAP!*

WELL, NO MORE! YOU SHALL PREPARE ANOTHER *WELL-RESEARCHED* REPORT ON THE HISTORICAL FIGURE OF YOUR CHOICE--*EXCLUDING* THE MAN WHO INVENTED THE TOILET.

THOMAS J. CRAPPER?

I KNOW WHO INVENTED THE TOILET, SIMPSON!!

YOU WILL DELIVER AN ORAL PRESENTATION IN FRONT OF THE *ENTIRE* SCHOOL NEXT WEEK AT OUR MONTHLY *"WHAT BART DID WRONG AND WHY YOU SHOULDN'T DO IT"* ASSEMBLY.

AND, SO YOU SHALL NEVER FORGET YOUR HISTORICAL TRANSGRESSION, YOU WILL PREPARE AND DELIVER SAID REPORT WITH YOUR *FATHER*...

HOMER J. SIMPSON!

I HAVE TO DO *WHAT*?

HOMER, YOU GOTTA WEAR A *RADIATION SUIT* WHEN YOU GO INTO THE CORE.

LENNY, THAT'S JUST A *GUIDELINE*.

ANGER!

SECTOR 7-G

RIIIING!

YEEEELLO. WHAT IS IT BOY? I HAVE TO DO *WHAT*?

WELL, CAN WE DO THE GUY WHO INVENTED THE TOILET?

D'OH.

LATER...

WHAT'RE WE GONNA DO? WHAT'RE WE GONNA DO? I DON'T KNOW HISTORY! I DON'T EVEN KNOW WHAT FREAKIN' *COUNTRY* WE'RE IN ANYMORE! THE UNITED STATES? AMERICA? LAND O' LAKES?

I DON'T WANNA LOOK AT BOOKS! *I DON'T WANNA LOOK AT BOOKS! I CAN'T BREATHE!*

UNCLE DAD'S SOUTHERN-STYLE CARAMEL TUB
Now with ice cream!

DAD, I KNOW WHAT YOU'RE GOING THROUGH, BUT YOU CAN'T *PANIC*. WHAT WE HAVE TO DO IS TAKE OUR MIND OFF OF IT. *EASE* INTO THE WORK...

"EUGENE V. DEBS AND HIS UNHOLY VAMPIRE UNION!" "BURIED ALIVE BY ELIZABETH CADY STANTON!" "ED MEESE--KING MAGGOT!" WE HIT THE *JACKPOT*, DAD! WE COULD DO *EIGHT* REPORTS ON THIS STUFF!

OF COURSE IT'S A GOOD IDEA, MARGE! THE BOY HAS NEVER BEEN *MORE INTERESTED* IN SCHOOLWORK. THEY SHOULD HORRIFY *ALL* HIS SUBJECTS: MENTALLY-SCARRING MATH! SKIN-CRAWLING SCIENCE! HIGHLY-TRAUMATIC ENGLISH!

DAD, WHO ARE YOU TALKING TO?

OH, I THOUGHT THAT WAS MARGE. WELL, IT *HAD* TO BE SAID.

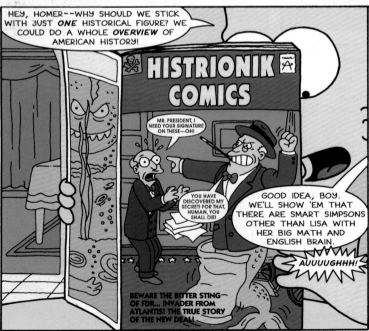

HEY, HOMER--WHY SHOULD WE STICK WITH JUST *ONE* HISTORICAL FIGURE? WE COULD DO A WHOLE *OVERVIEW* OF AMERICAN HISTORY!

HISTRIONIK COMICS

MR. PRESIDENT, I NEED YOUR SIGNATURE ON THESE--OH!

YOU HAVE DISCOVERED MY SECRET! FOR THAT, HUMAN, YOU SHALL DIE!

GOOD IDEA, BOY. WE'LL SHOW 'EM THAT THERE ARE SMART SIMPSONS OTHER THAN LISA WITH HER BIG MATH AND ENGLISH BRAIN.

AUUUUGHHH!

BEWARE THE BITTER STING OF FDR... INVADER FROM ATLANTIS! THE TRUE STORY OF THE NEW DEAL!

BILLY BEER WAS ORIGINALLY BREWED TO TURN MILLIONS INTO *WEREWOLVES!*

OHMIGOD, OHMIGOD, OHMIGOD!! I'M AT RISK!

...ALL I GOTTA REMEMBER IS THAT GEORGE WASHINGTON CHOPPED UP THE CHERRY SALESMAN...

ALTHOUGH SEEING YOU HUMILIATED BEFORE THE ENTIRE SCHOOL WOULD GIVE ME A GREAT SENSE OF ACCOMPLISHMENT, I'M GLAD TO SEE YOU'VE *PREPARED,* BART...

...AS I'VE INVITED SOME VERY *IMPORTANT* GUESTS.

"AFTER LISTENING TO THEIR CONCERNS AT THE CITY'S ANNUAL 'WHAT BART DID THIS YEAR AND HOW WE CAN MAKE SURE THOSE INCIDENTS NEVER REPEAT' CONFERENCE, I HAVE INVITED SUCH LUMINARIES AS:

"...THE GUFF-INTOLERANT *MAYOR QUIMBY*..."

"...OBSCENITY-SENSITIVES *MAUDE AND NED FLANDERS*..."

"...*REVEREND LOVEJOY* AND HIS ALARMIST WIFE, *HELEN*..."

"...YOUR FATHER'S PERPETUALLY-ANGRY BOSS *MR. BURNS* AND HIS DITHERING LICKSPITTLE, *WAYLON SMITHERS*..."

"...THE RELENTLESS LAWMAN *CHIEF WIGGUM*..."

"...AND SPRINGFIELD'S FAVORITE NO-NONSENSE JEWISH LEADER, *RABBI HYMAN KRUSTOFSKI*."

ARE WE SUPPOSED TO BE SCARED AND OR IMPRESSED? YOU TELL ALL THOSE POLITICAL AND RELIGIOUS LEADERS TO PREPARE TO HAVE THEIR BUTTS KICKED BY *HISTORY!*

DON'T TAP ME.

OKAY.

79

MOST OF YOU HAVE GROWN UP USING THE TOOTHPASTE *"THEY"* WANT YOU TO USE. DRINKING WHAT *"THEY"* MAKE SURE WINS THE VARIOUS COLA CHALLENGES. LEARNING THE HISTORY *"THEY"* WANT YOU TO KNOW.

BUT, WHAT IF WE WERE TO INFORM YOU THAT *"THEY"* AREN'T TELLING YOU THE *WHOLE STORY?*

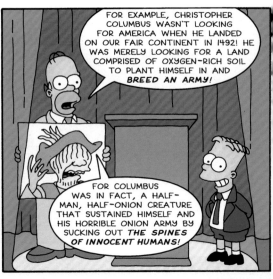

FOR EXAMPLE, CHRISTOPHER COLUMBUS WASN'T LOOKING FOR AMERICA WHEN HE LANDED ON OUR FAIR CONTINENT IN 1492! HE WAS MERELY LOOKING FOR A LAND COMPRISED OF OXYGEN-RICH SOIL TO PLANT HIMSELF IN AND *BREED AN ARMY!*

FOR COLUMBUS WAS IN FACT, A HALF-MAN, HALF-ONION CREATURE THAT SUSTAINED HIMSELF AND HIS HORRIBLE ONION ARMY BY SUCKING OUT *THE SPINES OF INNOCENT HUMANS!*

MOM?

URRRMMMM...

THIRTY SECONDS LATER...

SORRY, FOLKS. ¡SOB!: I'D FROWN WITH THE REST OF YOU, BUT I JUST CAN'T STOP CRYIN'... ¡SOB!:

SAY GOODBYE TO YOUR DADDY, LITTLE LADY. HE'S GOIN' AWAY FOR A *LONG* TIME.

WHY? WHAT'S THE CHARGE?

AFTER LOU TOOK HIM OUT WITH THAT FIFTY POUND SANDBAG, WE FOUND *THESE COMICS* ON HIS PERSON.

SO *WHAT?*

"SO WHAT." ¡HRMPH¡. THAT'S WHAT I'D SAY, TOO, IF THOSE COMICS WEREN'T *OBSCENE!*

IN *SPRINGFIELD*, IF YOU'RE GONNA CALL CHRISTOPHER COLUMBUS A SPINE-EATING ONIONMAN, YOU'RE GONNA HAVE YOUR DIRTY LAUNDRY GONE THROUGH...

...AND I GUARANTEE WE'LL FIND SOMETHING PRETTY BADLY SOILED. THIS TIME, WE FOUND COMIC BOOK CONTRABAND WORTHY OF A BIG-TIME INDICTMENT. *BOO YAH!*

YOU BETTER START GIVIN' US SOME ANSWERS, DICK TRACY, OR ELSE. THIS IS A TOWN THAT TAKES OBSCENITY PRETTY *&%@&$ SERIOUSLY.

HEY!

WATCH THE *LANGUAGE* PIGGY!

OH, GEE. *SORRY* ABOUT THAT. WON'T HAPPEN AGAIN.

SO, WHAT'RE *YOU* IN FOR, STRANGER?

MR. SIMPSON, ARE YOU CAUGHT IN A *PARALLEL UNIVERSE*? PERHAPS ONE IN WHICH YOU ARE *NOT* A BRAINLESS AUTOMATON? THE CONSTABLES BROUGHT ME IN BECAUSE THEY BELIEVE THE COMICS I SOLD YOU ARE *OBSCENE*.

OMIGOD, THEY GOT *YOU TOO*!

MR. SIMPSON, YOU *TOLD* THEM IT WAS ME. WHY DIDN'T YOU *TELL ME* YOU WERE DOING A HISTORY REPORT IN THE FIRST PLACE? I WOULDN'T HAVE GIVEN YOU THAT HISTRIONIK *PABLUM!* I WOULD HAVE STEERED YOU TOWARDS DOING A PROFILE ON JACK KIRBY, HARVEY KURTZMAN, OR THE INDOMITABLE DAVE "THE LIGHTER SIDE" BERG!

LISTEN TO ME CAREFULLY. WE HAVE TO STICK TOGETHER-- THEY'RE TRYING TO USE US AGAINST EACH OTHER, LIKE THEY DID TO KIRK AND SPOCK IN "AMOK TIME". I'M GOING TO BE REPRESENTING MYSELF, AND I SUGGEST THAT YOU LET ME REPRESENT YOU, TOO.

DO YOU HAVE ANY EXPERIENCE?

I'VE LAID WITNESS TO THE GREATEST CASES IN HISTORY; *"REVERSE FLASH V. THE FLASH," "THE TRIAL OF GALACTUS,"* AND EVERY LITIGATION EVER HANDLED BY *MARY WORTH*.

OOOOH!

HELLO, I'M KENT BROCKMAN AND I'M HORRIBLY *DISGUSTED*. THE OBJECT OF MY REVULSION? COMIC BOOKS.

ONCE, THEY WERE A SACRED BASTION OF *INNOCENCE*, GIVING US PULPY, NON-SMUTTY HAPPINESS FOR ONLY A NICKEL. BUT NOW, IMAGINE IF THOSE WONDERFUL KATZENJAMMER KIDS HAD GROWN UP TO BE *SKINHEADS* AND SWEET LITTLE NANCY, A CHEAP *HARLOT*... THAT'S WHAT'S HAPPENING TODAY.

FINE, YOU SAY, SKINHEADS AND HARLOTS HAVE BEEN THE FODDER FOR MANY A PRIME-TIME SITCOM FOR YEARS. NOT SO FINE, SAY I. FOR THESE COMICS, THESE *HISTRIONIK COMICS*, CROSS THE LINE FROM THE WORLD OF OBJECTIONABLE ENTERTAINMENT INTO THE DARK, STICKY DOMAIN OF OBSCENE MATERIAL.

AND TO PROVE IT, WE SHOWED COPIES OF THESE HORRIFYING ISSUES TO YOUNG, IMPRESSIONABLE CHILDREN TO PROVE HOW THEY INFLICT SUDDEN, PERMANENT DAMAGE TO THEIR FRAGILE, MUSH-FILLED EGGSHELL SKULLS.

"THEIR REACTIONS RANGED FROM SUDDEN, PROJECTILE REPULSION..."

"...TO SIMPLE DENIAL OF THE HORRORS WITNESSED..."

IT TASTES BAD.

"...TO INTENSE TRAUMA... SOME EVEN QUESTIONING THE VERY EXISTENCE OF GOD."

¿SOB!¿ I JUST ¿SOB!¿ CAN'T STOP ¿SOB!¿ CRYING...

GOD? ARE YOU THERE? IF YOU EXIST, PLEASE MAKE THIS STOP.

AND WHAT OF THE *MEN* WHO HAVE BROUGHT THIS PLAGUE OF PRURIENCE UPON OUR FAIR COMMUNITY? WELL, THE NUCLEAR PLANT EMPLOYEE WHO WAS A SICK, STEADY CUSTOMER AND THE COMIC STORE OWNER WHO WAS HIS SOULLESS SUPPLIER WERE *RELEASED* ON BAIL TODAY, AWAITING TRIAL.

THANKS TO THE UNITED STATES CONSTITUTION, THESE *SCUM* ARE ACTUALLY WALKING OUR OWN, ONLY LIGHTLY-SCUMMED CITY STREETS.

I SIMPLY DON'T KNOW WHAT'S MORE *PERVERTED*: THESE HORRIBLE CONNOISSEURS OF TRIPEY YUCK OR OUR AMERICAN LEGAL SYSTEM. THIS IS KENT BROCKMAN, STILL DISGUSTED OUTSIDE OF SPRINGFIELD ELEMENTARY.

HOMER, YOU'VE BEEN OUT OF JAIL FOR ALMOST AN *HOUR*. YOU CAN TAKE THAT *OFF* NOW.

BUT IT'S JUST SO *COMFORTABLE*! THERE'S NO RESTRICTIVE WAISTLINE!

HOMER, I DON'T GET IT. WHAT DID WE DO *WRONG*?

CLICK!

BUFFY--*SLAY* IT! SLAY IT *NOW*! OH, PLEASE HURRY! THERE'S A SALE AT *STRUCTURE*!

WELL, KIDS, WHAT I DID WAS PURCHASE EIGHTEEN COMIC BOOKS THAT THE GOVERNMENT THINKS ARE TOO DISGUSTING TO BE READ BY *ANY LIVING THING*.

WAIT; YOU'RE SAYING THAT I COULD WRITE SOME WORDS AND DRAW SOME PICTURES *SO GROSS* THAT IT'D BE A CRIME TO *LOOK* AT THEM?

UH-HUH.

CLICK!

ALLY, YOU CAN'T ASK HIM OUT! HE'S A *FEDERAL JUDGE* ABOUT TO SEND YOUR CLIENT TO THE *ELECTRIC CHAIR*!

SKRITCH SKRITCH

UH-HUH... I DON'T THINK HE'S WEARING ANYTHING UNDER THAT ROBE EXCEPT THOSE REALLY NICE ITALIAN SHOES.

HOW 'BOUT THIS?

NO.

THIS?

NO.

THIS?

NO.

FLIP FLIP FLIP

THIS?

WE HAVE A *WINNER*! NOW, *THAT'S* THE KIND OF STUFF THAT SENT ME TO THE BIG HOUSE!

DAD, THE FIRST AMENDMENT OF THE UNITED STATES CONSTITUTION SAYS THAT CONGRESS SHALL MAKE NO LAW ABRIDGING THE FREEDOM OF SPEECH OR FREEDOM OF THE PRESS.

IT WAS YOUR *CONSTITUTIONAL RIGHT* TO BUY THOSE GHASTLY COMICS JUST AS IT'S BART'S RIGHT TO DRAW THIS...

GAAAAURRRK.

YES, THAT IS CORRECT. HIS *RIGHT*. AND PERHAPS THEY ALLOW YOU TO ACTUALLY EXERCISE THIS RIGHT SOMEWHERE NEAR THE PLANET QUORSHAN-8.

I AM THE PROPRIETOR OF THE *ANDROID'S DUNGEON*, AND I AM HERE TO DISCUSS *LEGAL STRATEGY* WITH MY CO-DEFENDANT.

WHO--

BUT HOW DID YOU GET IN?

AFTER USING A MOTHER BOX TO FLING MYSELF INTO THE *FUTURE*, I ACCESSED RECORDS OF WHAT TRANSPIRED IN OUR TRIAL. I THEN SPENT SOME TIME WORKING FOR THE FEDERATION, GATHERING EXPERIENCE WHILE TRYING COURT-MARTIALS.

FINALLY, I USED AN EXPERIMENTAL PROCEDURE ON THE TRANSPORTER ROOM'S SENSOR ARRAY, ALLOWING ME TO BE BEAMED BACK HERE, INTO YOUR LIVING ROOM.

OKAY, YOUR FRONT DOOR WAS AJAR. SO UM, LET'S GET TO WORK.

OOOH! I JUST *LOVE* WHAT YOU DID WITH YOUR *PRISON UNIFORM!*

I JUST MADE SOME MINOR ALTERATIONS. THIS IS THE MOST COMFORTABLE PIECE OF CLOTHING I'VE EVER WORN! THERE'S NO RESTRICTIVE WAISTLINE.

SPRING JAIL

SPRINGFIELD JAIL

SINCE THE DAWN OF TIME, GOVERNMENT HAS *HATED* COMIC BOOK SHOPS. NOT ONLY DO COMIC BOOKS HELP FOSTER A THIRST FOR *TRUTH* AND *JUSTICE*, BUT THEY ARE ALSO A FORUM FOR IMPORTANT *IDEAS*, SUCH AS THE NOW-CLASSIC YARN, *RADIOACTIVE MAN VS. THE LIVING BONG.*

SPRINGFIELD HAS BEEN AN ESPECIALLY *INHOSPITABLE ENVIRONMENT* FOR THE MEDIUM. AFTER THIS ONE-PANEL GAG WAS PUBLISHED IN THE SPRINGFIELD SHOPPER, MAYOR QUIMBY WENT ON TO BAN ALL POLITICAL CARTOONS.

IN 1980, WHEN A YOUNG TYKE *CHOKED* ON A COPY OF *SECRET WARS #4*, THE CITY SHUT DOWN *"THE GEEKERY"*, SAYING THAT COMICS WERE UNSAFE FOR THE READING PUBLIC.

TWO YEARS LATER, *"SEQUENTIAL ART'S"* WAS RUN OUT OF BUSINESS BECAUSE THE CITY THOUGHT THAT *THE FLASH* WAS ABOUT A HERO THAT BESTED HIS FOES BY *EXPOSING HIMSELF.*

DIAMOND JOE: THE MUSICAL
Wine, women, and wrong (doing)!

Turns out DIAMOND JOE was a CUBIC ZIRCONIA.

CLOSED BY ORDER OF THE CITY

The Geekery

Springfield Shopper
Super-nudie nightmare nixed

THEY THINK THEY CAN PUSH US AROUND TO FURTHER THEIR OWN TWISTED AGENDAS AND OPEN RETAIL SPACE FOR *COFFEEHOUSES* THAT BESMIRCH THE NAMES OF BELOVED *BATTLESTAR GALACTICA* CHARACTERS.

ONE BY ONE, MY COMPETITION HAS BEEN CLOSED DOWN--NOT BY MY SUPERIOR RACKING AND MARKETING, BUT BY A TECHNOCRATIC, OPPRESSIVE GOVERNMENT. I KNEW ONE DAY, THEY WOULD COME AFTER ME. BUT I AM READY.

LIS, DAD IS THREE STEPS AWAY FROM THE *STATE PEN!* WE GOTTA *DO* SOMETHING.

BART, THIS ISN'T LIKE FINDING A BOOK OF SPELLS TO REVERSE A ZOMBIE CURSE OR READING THROUGH ANCIENT JUDAIC TEXTS TO FIND ARGUMENTS TO JUSTIFY CLOWNING-- THIS IS *OBSCENITY LAW.* IT'S GOING TO TAKE SOME *TIME!*

THE *LAWYERS*, THE *GOVERNMENT* OFFICIALS, THAT HORRIBLE *"UP WITH PEOPLE"* ORGANIZATION--I KNOW THEIR TACTICS. THEY ARE A SUPERSTITIOUS, COWARDLY LOT, FRAGGIN' BASTICHES ONE AND ALL. *THEY* DON'T JUST FIGHT IN THE *COURTROOM*, AND NEITHER SHOULD *WE!*

MR. SIMPSON...

...PLEASE GIVE MY FEDERATION TORCH BACK AND TURN THE LIGHT BACK *ON!*

OKAY.

OUR FIRST PRIORITY IS *SPIN*. IF WE HAVE ANY HOPE OF WINNING THIS CASE, WE HAVE TO MANIPULATE THE MEDIA, WHICH HAS PORTRAYED US AS MONSTERS...

...INTO PORTRAYING US AS HUMANOID *NON-MONSTERS*, OR AT THE VERY LEAST, *ROMULANS*. WE NEED TO TAKE IT TO THE STREETS.

NOW SIGNING: Two Overweight, Innocent Men Accused of Perversion. & "BASEBALL CARDS"

OH, CROM. THIS IS WORSE THAN MY WESLEY CRUSHER COSMIC CLAMBAKE LAST AUGUST. BY THE END OF THE AFTERNOON, WILL WHEATON WAS SO *DEJECTED* THAT HE WALKED OVER TO THE KRUSTYBURGER AND TOOK A JOB AS *ASSISTANT MANAGER*. ALL IS LOST.

WE CAN'T GIVE UP YET! I HAVE A FAMILY AND MOE TO THINK ABOUT, AND YOU HAVE YOUR LEGIONS OF PIMPLE-FACED NERDS! THEY'RE USING TV AGAINST *US*, SO WHY DON'T WE USE IT AGAINST *THEM!*

WE'LL PUT ON AN AD WITH DY-NO-MITE CLASSIC ROCK AND GIRLS IN BIKINIS AND TALKING ALLIGATORS THAT SAY "HOMER J. SIMPSON AND...UH, THAT GUY WHO OWNS THE COMIC BOOK STORE ARE NOT PERVERTS!"

NOW *THAT* IS AN IDEA! BUT WE'LL NEED MONEY.

BAMM!

I'M CALLING THE PUBLISHERS OF HISTRIONIK COMICS FOR FINANCIAL ASSISTANCE IN OUR CAUSE. AFTER ALL, *THEY'RE* THE ONES THAT PUT US *IN* THIS MESS.

MOMENTS LATER...

THEY DENIED EVER PUBLISHING THE BOOKS, CLAIMING ONLY TO PRODUCE "LEON MEOWY," THE ADVENTURES OF A SWEET LITTLE KITTEN THAT'S ALWAYS GETTING HIS ABSENT-MINDED OWNER OUT OF ALL SORTS OF CRAZY MISADVENTURES.

OKAY, SO WE CAN'T DO THE AD. BUT I HAVE A *BRILLIANT* IDEA THAT'LL GET THE WORD OUT FOR ALMOST NOTHING.

WHAT I'VE SEEN AND WHAT I'VE SMELLED-- IT'S *HORRIBLE!*

I AM NOT A FREAK

HOMER, WE ARE TRYING TO CONVINCE PEOPLE WE ARE *NOT* SICKOS! WHY ARE YOU *NAKED* AND *RUBBING CRISCO* ALL OVER YOUR BODY?

I WAS HOT AND I RAN OUT OF SUNTAN LOTION. GEEZ, SAW-*REE* MR. SANDWICH BOARD REGULATION KING.

I'M NORMAL, I SWEAR IT

HONK IF YOU HATE BEING CAST AS A DEVIANT BY A SENSATIONALISTIC MEDIA

GOOD MORNING EVERYONE, COURT IS NOW IN SESSION. BEFORE WE START, I'D LIKE TO THANK *"SPRINGFIELDERS FOR CHILDREN AND FAMILIES AND WELL-BEHAVED PETS"* FOR THE WONDERFUL *FRUIT BASKET* THEY SENT ME THIS MORNING.

HANG 'EM HIGH, YOUR HONOR!

S.F.C.A.F. A.W.B.P

S.F.C.A.F. A.W.B.P

S.F.C.A.F. A.W.B.P

S.F.C.A. A.W.B

WELL, IT'S GOING TO BE UP TO THE JURY, BUT I'LL SEE WHAT I CAN DO. DEFENSE, BEGIN YOUR OPENING STATEMENT.

MR. SIMPSON, PREPARE TO BE DAZZLED.

SPRINGFIELD JAIL

PUNY HUMANS, WHEN WILL YOU LEARN? HULK *STRONGER* THAN YOU. HULK *SMARTER* THAN YOU. HULK *SMASH* YOU.

OF COURSE, I AM NOT THE HULK, THE HULK IS THE *TRUTH*. BUT YOU *ARE* THE *PUNY HUMANS*. WHAT'S WORSE, YOU'RE PUNY HUMANS THAT HAVE *DELUDED* YOURSELVES INTO THINKING THAT YOU ARE *FIT* TO PASS JUDGMENT LIKE THE *GUARDIANS OF THE GALAXY, GALACTUS,* OR EVEN, *KLAATU!*

ARE YOU ALL SO WITHOUT BIAS? AS IF YOU WERE *SHIELDED* FROM THIS WORLD BY YOUR OWN *BACTA TANKS,* SAFE AND SOUND FROM THE *RANCORS* AND *YAMBARS* OF INFLUENCE THAT SURELY CLOUD YOUR JUDGEMENT!

YOU ARE NOT IMPARTIAL *DATAS, WATCHERS,* OR EVEN *BEYONDERS.* YOU ARE *SKRULLS, CYLONS,* AND MEMBERS OF THE *DRACONIAN EMPIRE,* FLAWED IN DISPOSITIONS AND THOUGHT PATTERNS.

SPRINGFIELD JAIL

YOUR HONOR, I BELIEVE WE REQUIRE SOME SORT OF *TRANSLATION*.

DOES ANYONE SPEAK... THAT LANGUAGE HE JUST USED?

JOHWI'VAD MAMUGHLAH.

THAT WAS KLINGON FOR, "WE CAN TRANSLATE, YOUR HONOR."

...THEY SPOKE IN *GOBBLEDY-GEEK* ALL DAY, REFERRING TO ALIENS, SUPERHEROES, AND JAPANESE MONSTERS TO MAKE THEIR CONVOLUTED POINTS. THEIR REFERENCES TO THE *HISTRIONIK* COMIC BOOKS MADE SEVERAL JURORS PHYSICALLY ILL, AND HOMER SIMPSON, MISTAKING IT FOR A BATHROOM, *RELIEVED HIMSELF* IN THE JUROR'S COAT CLOSET.

WOULD YOU SAY IT'S NOT LOOKING *GOOD* FOR THE DEFENSE?

BART, I'VE LOOKED AT FEDERAL CASES RIGHT DOWN TO THE LOCAL LEVEL. I THINK WE'RE IN TROUBLE.

LISA, WHAT USE ARE SUPERIOR RESEARCH SKILLS AND A GREAT VOCABULARY IF YOU CAN'T SPRING YOUR DAD FROM AN OBSCENITY CHARGE?

I'D SAY THEY SHOULD PREPARE FOR PRISON LIFE.

I'D AGREE. THEY SHOULD SPEND THE NEXT FEW DAYS USING CIGARETTES AS CURRENCY, JUST TO GET THE HANG OF IT.

ALL THESE CASES--"DOG-EARED DAVE V. CALIFORNIA," "BATTLESTAR COMICBOOK-SHOPTICA V. TEXAS," AND "EVERY COMIC READER IN AMERICA V. OKLAHOMA"--RESULTED IN CONVICTIONS. THE DEFENDANTS JUST COULDN'T GET THE JURY TO STOP THINKING ABOUT THE *SENSATIONAL ASPECTS* OF THE CASE AND START THINKING ABOUT THE *FIRST AMENDMENT.*

JUR-EE?

JURY! THEY'RE THE PEOPLE WHO SIT IN THE JURY BOX AND DECIDE THE CASE.

OH. I JUST THOUGHT THOSE WERE THE PEOPLE WITH THE *GOOD* SEATS.

BART, THE FACT THAT EVERYONE IS ENTITLED UNDER LAW TO A SPEEDY TRIAL BEFORE A FAIR, IMPARTIAL JURY OF THEIR PEERS IS ONE OF THE MOST BASIC PRECEPTS OF AMERICAN LIFE! WHERE HAVE YOU *BEEN* DURING SOCIAL STUDIES CLASS?

READING COMICS, MOSTLY. JUST BE HAPPY I KNOW WHAT THE WORD "PEER" MEANS.

WAITAMINUTE...

MR. SIMPSON, THE TRIAL IS NOT GOING *WELL.* THE *JUDGE* DOESN'T LIKE US, THE *JURY* DOESN'T LIKE US, AND THE *STENOGRAPHER* HURLED HER *MACHINE* AT YOU DURING THE MIDDLE OF YOUR TESTIMONY. I THINK WE NEED A NEW STRATEGY. FORTUNATELY, I HAVE ONE.

SHE SAID IT *SLIPPED.*

HOMER! FLEEING TO COSTA RICA IS *NOT* THE ANSWER!

THERE'S ALL SORTS OF *AMERICAN FACTORIES* DOWN THERE! AUTO PLANTS, SOUP CANNERIES, AMERICAN FLAG MILLS! I'LL GET A JOB AND WHEN I GET SETTLED, I'LL *SEND* FOR YOU!

CHIPPO BUSHEL

CHIPPO BUSHEL

SPRINGFIELD T...

AN OIL DRUM OF TUBB

HOMER, THOSE JOBS PAY *EIGHTY CENTS* AN HOUR.

HOMER, *WAIT!*

YES, MARGE, BUT HOUSES ONLY COST TWELVE THOUSAND DOLLARS!

BULK CHICHARONES

18 Pounds of Puffs (cheese variety)

I THINK WE HAVE A DEFENSE.

THE NEXT MORN...

DURING THIS TRIAL, THE DEFENSE HAS SICKENED, ANGERED, ANNOYED, AND CAUSED ONE JUROR'S APPENDIX TO *BURST*. THEY NOW WANT TO HAVE A TEN-YEAR-OLD CHILD DELIVER THEIR CLOSING STATEMENT.

AT THIS POINT, I SAY *WHY NOT?* DEFENSE, YOU MAY PROCEED.

MEMBERS OF THE JURY, I STAND BEFORE YOU, A *GEEK*.

;GASP!;

MY *WORD!*

ER-AH, WHAT?

THOSE MEN OVER THERE READ AND COLLECT COMIC BOOKS. SO DO *THOSE* MEN.

DID ANY OF YOU EVEN KNOW COMIC BOOKS WERE *STILL PUBLISHED* WHEN YOU BECAME JURORS? HAVE ANY OF YOU BEEN INTO A COMIC BOOK STORE? MEMBERS OF THE JURY, DO YOU EVEN KNOW WHO OL' *BOLTHEAD* IS? HOW ABOUT *ABIN-SUR? BROTHER VOODOO?* DON'T WAIT FOR THE TRANSLATION--JUST ANSWER THE QUESTION!

TRANSLATION

I READ ONLY THE CLASSICS AND BIOGRAPHIES OF OTHER CLOWN SIDEKICKS.

WHO *SAYS* I DON'T KNOW COMICS? *AHHHR!* RAISED UPON THE HILARIOUS ADVENTURES OF *GARFIELD AND ODIE* WAS I!

THIS *"BROTHER VOODOO."* DOES HE HAVE A *WEBSITE?*

YOUR HONOR, ACCORDING TO MY LITTLE SISTER, OUR JUDICIAL SYSTEM IS BASED ON THE RIGHT OF THE ACCUSED TO BE JUDGED BY A JURY OF THEIR PEERS. MR. JUDGEGUY, I SUBMIT TO YOU THAT *NONE* OF THE MEMBERS OF THIS JURY ARE THE DEFENDANTS' PEERS!

THEY ARE NOT COMIC GEEKS. THEY AREN'T EVEN *SCI-FI FANS.* THEY, YOUR HONOR, ARE *BLAND CIVILIANS!* YOU WANT TO JUSTLY TRY THESE MEN--THEN PACK THAT JURY BOX WITH NERDS! IT'S THAT *SIMPLE,* YOUR HONOR. I REST MY CASE.

IN CONCORDANCE WITH THE SPRINGFIELD LITIGATION PLAY IT BY EAR ACT, I SAY... OKAY. WE'LL GIVE IT A SHOT WITH GEEKS.

BUH?

FOUR DAYS LATER...

WE, THE JURY, FIND THE DEFENDANTS... *INNOCENT* OF ALL OBSCENITY CHARGES.

FREE HAL JORDAN

LONG LIVE THE LEGION

I REALLY, REALLY, REALLY WANT TO BELIEVE

All Agog Over Magog

METROPOLIS U

OH, THANK THE MAKER... ER, I MEAN, THANK GOODNESS!

HUZZAH FOR MY WISE BRETHREN!

YOU *DID* IT, BOY! YOU *DID* IT!

HOWEVER, THE JURY DID CHOOSE TO INFLICT ADDITIONAL CHARGES, WHICH, ALTHOUGH UNCONSTITUTIONAL, ARE PERMITTED ON SEVERAL FEDERATION PLANETS.

DEFENDANT ONE, PLEASE RISE.

HUH?

WHA?

I REALLY, REALLY, REALLY WANT TO BELIEVE

LONG LIVE THE LEGION

All Agog Over M

WHOOZA?

METROPOLIS U

WE FIND YOU GUILTY OF CONDESCENSION, COVER-CRINKLING, PRICE-GOUGING, USING HIGHLY ACIDIC BOARDS, SELLING COMICS SOILED BY BURRITO DRIPPINGS, RUINING THE ENDING TO THE "DEATH OF SUPERMAN," AND BRIBING THE MANAGER OF THE TOY AISLE AT TRY N' SAVE TO BUY UP ALL THE NEW "HIP-HOP YO! YO! YODA" ACTION FIGURES.

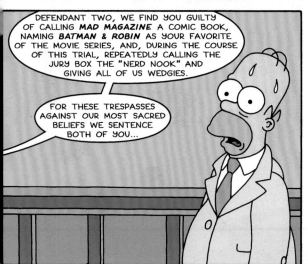

DEFENDANT TWO, WE FIND YOU GUILTY OF CALLING *MAD MAGAZINE* A COMIC BOOK, NAMING *BATMAN & ROBIN* AS YOUR FAVORITE OF THE MOVIE SERIES, AND, DURING THE COURSE OF THIS TRIAL, REPEATEDLY CALLING THE JURY BOX THE "NERD NOOK" AND GIVING ALL OF US WEDGIES.

FOR THESE TRESPASSES AGAINST OUR MOST SACRED BELIEFS WE SENTENCE BOTH OF YOU...

...TO *PUBLIC HANGING!!*

G

AISLE 1000

GEEZ, IT'S HOT. I DON'T KNOW ABOUT *YOU*, BUT I'M TAKING OFF MY PANTS.

IC

TWO OVERWEIGHT MEN ACQUITTED OF OBSCENITY WELCOME YOU TO **CLOSE ENCOUNTERS OF THE COMIC BOOK KIND IX**

EXIT

CONGO COMICS

RARE!

SUPER RARE!

NOW SIGNING! COMIC BOOK LEGAL SCHOLAR Bart Simpson ROOM 7A-B

THE END.

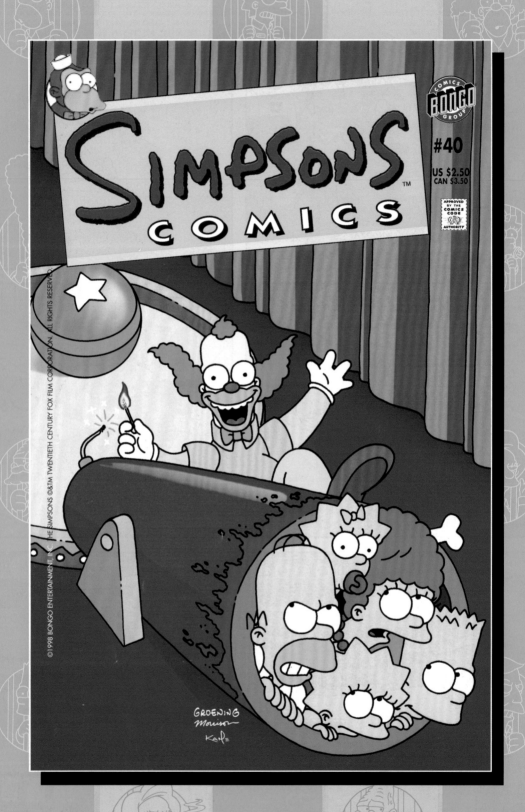

HOMER SIMPSON! WHAT ARE YOU DING-DIDDLY *DOING* HERE? IT'S THREE O'CLOCK IN THE MORNING!

THAT *YOU* HAD A BAR WITH A POOL TABLE TOO, AND *YOUR* PLACE *NEVER* CLOSES!

BUT MY DOOR *WAS* CLOSED--AND *LOCKED!* HOW DID YOU GET IN?

I'LL FIELD THAT QUESHTION. *SHKELETON KEYS* TO *EVERY* HOUSH IN TOWN!

SOON...

HOMER, I'M SURE THIS *IS* THE BEST IDEA YOU'VE EVER HAD, ⸢YAWN⸣ BUT CAN'T IT WAIT TILL MORNING?

BUT JUST *THINK* ABOUT IT, MARGE! OUR VERY OWN REC ROOM, JUST LIKE FLANDERS... RIGHT HERE IN OUR BASEMENT! WE'LL HAVE A POOL TABLE, AND A JUKEBOX...AND A BAR, MARGE! A *BAR*, COMPLETE WITH ONE OF THOSE CUTE LITTLE PLASTIC DRUNK GUYS WHO DROP THEIR PANTS AND SHOOT WHISKEY INTO YOUR GLASS!

WHERE ARE WE GOING?

JUST FOLLOW ME. I WANT TO SHOW YOU SOMETHING.

SEE THIS MESS? THERE'S NOT EVEN ROOM FOR A *FOOSBALL GAME*, MUCH LESS A *BAR AND POOL TABLE*. I WON'T EVEN *THINK* ABOUT LETTING YOU BUILD YOUR LITTLE CLUBHOUSE UNTIL THIS BASEMENT IS CLEANED OUT--STARTING WITH THAT *OLMEC INDIAN HEAD!*

BUT MARGE, THAT WAS A GIFT FROM MY BOSS. SUPPOSE HE COMES OVER.

HE CAN'T EVEN REMEMBER YOUR NAME! WHAT MAKES YOU THINK HE'S GOING TO DROP IN FOR A VISIT?

I'M SORRY HOMER, BUT IF YOU WANT A REC ROOM, THAT THING HAS TO GO.

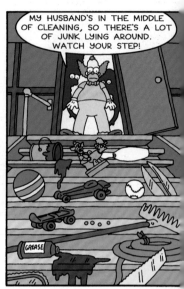

TELL *DR. HIBBERT* I HOPE HE RECOVERS FROM HIS *HYSTERECTOMY* SOON.

¡HEH, HEH! YOU BET! WELL, GOODBYE EVERYBODY!

GOODBYE, DOCTOR NICK!

OKAY KRUSTY, I KNOW ONE OF YOUR PHONY BALONEY ACTS WHEN I SEE IT. YOU'RE NOT REALLY HURT! YOU CAN TAKE A FALL LIKE THAT IN YOUR SLEEP! NOW, WHAT'S GOING ON?

THE PERFECT SET UP, *THAT'S WHAT!* WE'RE GONNA DO THE BIG SHOW FROM *HERE,* WHERE FAT TONY AND HIS GOONS CAN'T *FIND* ME!

PLUS, I CAN USE *THE SIMPSONS* AS MY *STOOGES!*

WHAT IF THEY REFUSE?

DO THE WORDS "*SLIP AND FALL LAWSUIT*" MEAN ANYTHING TO YOU?

"NOW, GET ON THE PHONE TO THE STUDIO AND HAVE THEM BRING THE WHOLE OPERATION OVER HERE. SETS, COSTUMES, PROPS, EQUIPMENT--*EVERYTHING!*"

HMM...*THAT'S* ODD. WHERE COULD THAT TRUCK BE GOING WITH ALL OF OUR STAGE FURNISHINGS? PERHAPS WE SHOULD FOLLOW IT AND FIND OUT.

DOWN WITH CLOWN!

KRUSTY IS A SCHNORRER!

ENOUGH WITH THE MISHEGOSS, ALREADY!

SAY, FAT TONY, AIN'T THAT KRUSTOFSKI'S BOYS TAILIN' THAT TRUCK?

A KEEN OBSERVATION, LEGS. I DO NOT LIKE THE LOOKS OF THIS.

RIGHT, BOSS!

LOUIE, FOLLOW THAT CAR.

WELL, IT LOOKS LIKE I'M STUCK HERE FOR THE DURATION! HEY KID, LET'S SEE WHAT'S ON THE TUBE WHILE *THE MOM-STER* FIXES ME SOMETHING TO EAT.

A REUBEN SANDWICH WOULD BE GREAT. SLICE THE CORNED BEEF *EXTRA* THIN BUT *LEAVE* THE FAT. AND MAKE SURE YOU USE *BROWN MUSTARD!*

YOU HEARD THE MAN, *MOM-STER!* CHOP, CHOP!

DING DONG!

HRRRRM. LISA, SEE IF YOU CAN FIND OUR *"GUEST"* SOMETHING TO SNACK ON WHILE I ANSWER THE DOOR.

OKAY, MOM-STER!

NOW, CUT THAT OUT!

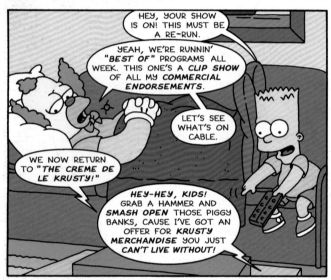

HEY, YOUR SHOW IS ON! THIS MUST BE A RE-RUN.

YEAH, WE'RE RUNNIN' *"BEST OF"* PROGRAMS ALL WEEK. THIS ONE'S A *CLIP SHOW* OF ALL MY *COMMERCIAL ENDORSEMENTS.*

LET'S SEE WHAT'S ON CABLE.

WE NOW RETURN TO *"THE CREME DE LE KRUSTY!"*

HEY-HEY, KIDS! GRAB A HAMMER AND *SMASH OPEN* THOSE PIGGY BANKS, CAUSE I'VE GOT AN OFFER FOR *KRUSTY MERCHANDISE* YOU JUST *CAN'T LIVE WITHOUT!*

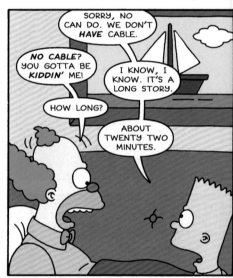

SORRY, NO CAN DO. WE DON'T *HAVE* CABLE.

NO CABLE? YOU GOTTA BE *KIDDIN'* ME!

I KNOW, I KNOW. IT'S A LONG STORY.

HOW LONG?

ABOUT TWENTY TWO MINUTES.

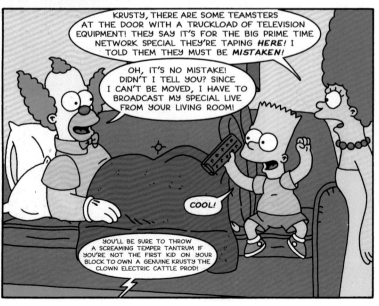

KRUSTY, THERE ARE SOME TEAMSTERS AT THE DOOR WITH A TRUCKLOAD OF TELEVISION EQUIPMENT! THEY SAY IT'S FOR THE BIG PRIME TIME NETWORK SPECIAL THEY'RE TAPING *HERE!* I TOLD THEM THEY MUST BE *MISTAKEN!*

OH, IT'S NO MISTAKE! DIDN'T I TELL YOU? SINCE I CAN'T BE MOVED, I HAVE TO BROADCAST MY SPECIAL LIVE FROM YOUR LIVING ROOM!

COOL!

YOU'LL BE SURE TO THROW A SCREAMING TEMPER TANTRUM IF YOU'RE NOT THE FIRST KID ON YOUR BLOCK TO OWN A GENUINE KRUSTY THE CLOWN ELECTRIC CATTLE PROD!

WHAT?!!

AND THERE'S *MORE!* YOU AND YOUR FAMILY WILL BE STANDING IN FOR MY USUAL CAST OF IDIOTS!

SHORTLY...

PLACES EVERYBODY! WE'RE COMING OUT OF COMMERCIAL!

HOLD ON! CORPORAL PUNISHMENT'S *MISSING!*

KRUSTY, I *CAN'T* HOLD! WE'RE *LIVE*...

...IN THREE...TWO... ONE...*YOU'RE ON!*

AW, *CRUD!*

HEH, HEH...ER, UH...BOY, I SURE WISH THAT FAT, LOUD-MOUTHED BUM OF A SERGEANT WAS HERE PLAYING THAT PIANO OFF-KEY, SO I COULD TELL HIM TO CUT IT OUT.

OH MAN, IT'S GONNA BE A LONG SKETCH.

HI, KRUSTY. NICE SHIRT. WANT A BEER?

HOMER, YOU BRAINDEAD *IDIOT!* WE'RE IN THE MIDDLE OF YOUR *SKETCH!*

UH, HEY THERE, *SARGE!* WHAT HAPPENED TO YOUR *UNIFORM?*

HUH? WHAT ARE YOU TALKING ABOU-- OH, *RIGHT!* THE *TV SHOW!*

CRASH!

SSSSSSSS

UNTIL...

OKAY EVERYBODY, TAKE FIVE WHILE I PERFORM MY FAMOUS ERNIE KOVACS RIP OFF-- ER, I MEAN *TRIBUTE*. THEN YOU GO RIGHT INTO THE *MA & PA SKETCH* WHILE I CHANGE MY COSTUME.

AND TELL THAT FREAKIN' KID TO PUT DOWN MY *BALL*! IT'S *NOT* A TOY!

BOY, KRUSTY SURE HAS MADE A QUICK RECOVERY.

IT'S ABOUT *TIME* SOMEBODY NOTICED THAT!

MOM, TELL *ELAYNE BOOSLER* TO QUIT HOGGIN' THE BATHROOM!

I HAVE *GRAVE MISGIVINGS* ABOUT DOING THIS NEXT SKETCH, MOM. SOMEHOW I DON'T THINK *THE OLMEC INDIAN GOD OF WAR* WOULD *APPRECIATE* BEING PORTRAYED AS A HILLBILLY'S OUTHOUSE.

I HAVEN'T HEARD HIM COMPLAIN ABOUT THE FACT THAT MOM'S BEEN *BEATING* OUR *CLOTHES* AGAINST HIM.

WELL, HE WORKS REALLY WELL ON STUBBORN STAINS!

I REALLY DON'T WANT TO DO THIS, MOM. *PLEASE* DON'T MAKE ME GO OUT THERE!

YEAH, ME TOO MOM! I'VE HAD IT UP TO *HERE* WITH THIS FARSHTINKENER SHOW!

THE BOY'S *RIGHT*! IT *IS* FARSHTINKENER!

I KNOW YOU'RE ALL UPSET. I AM TOO, BUT WE HAVE TO SEE THIS THROUGH TO THE END. WE CAN'T AFFORD A BIG LAWSUIT.

MAYBE *I* CAN HELP. I THINK KRUSTY NEEDS TO LEARN THAT HE CAN'T JUST USE OTHER PEOPLE TO AVOID PAYING FOR HIS OWN MISTAKES.

BUT HOW?

KRUSTY'S SIDEKICKS ARE STILL PICKETING OUT ON YOUR FRONT LAWN. I JUST BET THEY MIGHT BE WILLING TO HELP US. GO AHEAD AND START THE SKETCH, BUT BE PREPARED TO BAIL OUT.

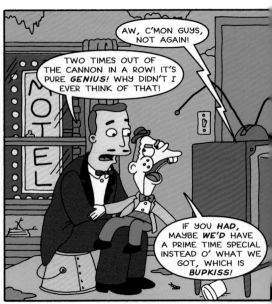

THE END

The Incredible Edible Exploits of

LARD LAD

WITH *CRULLER*, THE FRITTER CRITTER

IN SEARCH OF THE LOST DONUT HOLES!

AH, BEHOLD NATURE'S *PERFECT* FOOD -- THE *DONUT!!!*

HOW COULD *ANYTHING* BE CONSIDERED *PERFECT* WITH SUCH A BIG *HOLE* IN THE MIDDLE OF IT?

IF LARD LAD *STRETCHES* HIS *OVERALLS* ANY *TIGHTER,* THAT DONUT WON'T BE THE *ONLY* THING WITH A BIG *HOLE!*

SCOTT SHAW!

| SCRIPT AND PENCILS BY *SCOTT 'JELLY-FILLED' SHAW!* | INKS BY *TIM 'SPRINKLES' BAVINGTON* | LETTERS BY *CHRIS 'CRUMBY' UNGAR* | COLORS BY *NATHAN 'POWDERED SUGAR' KANE* | EDITS BY *BILL 'GLAZED' MORRISON* | LARD LAD'S BEST CUSTOMER *MATT GROENING* |

BUT CUPCAKE (MY SWEET BUT HALF-BAKED GIRLFRIEND), IT IS THAT SELFSAME *HOLE* THAT SUBLIMELY *TRANSFORMS* A MERE DEEP-FRIED SWEET BUN...

...INTO AN ETERNAL-YET-MYSTERIOUS *CIRCLE* WITHOUT *BEGINNING* OR *END* -- A VERITABLE *CIRCLE OF LIFE!*

GULP!

NOT TO MENTION A VERITABLE CIRCLE OF *HEART* ATTACKS!

I'M *IMPRESSED,* LARD LAD! I NEVER *SUSPECTED* YOU HAD SUCH A *PHILOSOPHICAL* BENT!

OH, THAT'S JUST A *SIDE-EFFECT* OF THE *MASSIVE SUGAR BUZZ* I GET AFTER EATING A FEW DOZEN *DONUTS!*

117

GET A WELL-ROUNDED LIFE! EAT LARD LAD DONUTS!

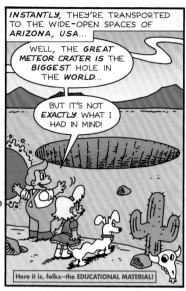

LARD LAD DONUTS ARE <u>LARDIER</u> DONUTS!

SIMPSONS COMICS ™

BONGO COMICS GROUP

#41

US $2.50
CAN $3.50

APPROVED BY THE COMICS CODE AUTHORITY

presents

"BART SIMPSON & THE KRUSTY BRAND FUN FACTORY"

GROENING
Morrison
Kerr

PFFFT! THAT IS *SO* LAST WEEK, MARGE.

KEEP IT DOWN, HOMEBOY. I WANT TO HEAR KRUSTY'S NEW COMMERCIAL.

HEY KIDS, TELL YOUR MOMS TO BUY CASES AND CASES OF *KRUSTY BRAND CHERRY SODA!*

AND IF SHE'S NOT AROUND, SAVE HER SOME TIME BY BORROWING ONE OF HER *CREDIT CARDS* AND DOING IT *YOURSELF!* WA-HOO-HOO-HOO-HUH!

HEY, HEY! IT'S LIKE A CHERRY PIE IN A BOTTLE, KIDS!

IT'S THE FIRST IN A LINE OF PRODUCTS FROM MY NEW *KRUSTY BRAND FUN FACTORY!*

I'M TIRED OF PEOPLE PUTTING MY NAME ON DEFECTIVE AND UNSAFE PRODUCTS! FROM NOW ON, I'M MAKING MY OWN!

KRUSTY'S G'DAY BIDET

KRUSTY BIKE IN A BOX

KRUSTY BRAND Baby Bum Powder

PORK JUICE

KRUSTY BRAND Cream Pie in a Can

KRUSTY Satellite with Launcher

KRUSTY Sings 'THE CHIPMUNKS'

EACH BEARING THE KRUSTY BRAND "SEAL OF SINCERITY."

KRUSTY'S INFLATABLE FRIEND

KRUSTY BRAND SEAL OF SINCERITY

My sincere apologies if you're not 100% satisfied.

WE INTERRUPT THIS COMMERCIAL FOR A SPECIAL ANNOUNCEMENT FROM KRUSTY THE CLOWN, LIVE AT MARTHA'S VINEYARD.

WHY I NEVER LAID A GLOVE ON THAT WOMAN... *WHAT?!?*

...OH, *THAT*... HEH, HEH... TO CELEBRATE MY NEW KRUSTY BRAND PRODUCTS, I'D LIKE TO ANNOUNCE *A KRUSTACULAR CONTEST!*

FOUR LUCKY KIDS AND THEIR LEGAL GUARDIANS OR PAROLE OFFICERS WILL WIN AN EXCITING GUIDED TOUR THROUGH THE KRUSTY BRAND FUN FACTORY (ADJACENT TO THE SCENIC SPRINGFIELD PRISON) LED BY *ME, KRUSTY THE CLOWN!*

SOMEWHERE OUT THERE ARE *FOUR GOLDEN STRAWS*, HIDDEN IN BOTTLES OF *KRUSTY'S CHERRY SODA!* TO WIN, JUST FIND ONE OF THESE FABULOUS, *GOLDEN STRAWS*. DID I MENTION THAT THEY'RE MADE OF REAL *GOLD?*

NO, HE DID NOT.

THIS IS KRUSTY WATCH '99. I'M KENT BROCKMAN, LIVE AT THE SPRINGFIELD MONSTROMART, WHERE RALPH WIGGUM HAS BECOME THE *FIRST* LUCKY OWNER OF A *GOLDEN STRAW!*

HEY, HEY! IT'S LIKE A CHERRY PIE IN A BOTTLE!

KRUSTY BRAND

SURPRISINGLY, THE YOUNG BOY WAS UNHINDERED BY THE CROWDS.

WE'RE ALMOST DONE HERE. COME ON! GIVE THE BOY SOME ROOM, YOU PEOPLE.

DADDY, MY NOSE SMELLS LIKE COUGH SYRUP!

TAPED EARLIER

LOUSY, STINKING, SELF-SERVING CIVIL SERVANTS! ALWAYS GETTING THE *GOLD MINE* WHILE I GET *THE SHAFT!*

GLUG GLUG GLUG!

GOOD HEAVENS! I'M NO DOCTOR, BUT I THINK YOUR FATHER HAS A BURST APPENDIX! THANK GOODNESS HE WAS NEAR HIS *LOVING FAMILY* WHEN THIS HAPPENED.

QUICK, KIDS, CALL 911!

MRRROW!

CHOKE!

COUGH!

ACK!

AW, MOM, THERE'S ONLY THREE STRAWS LEFT!

NOW, KIDS, YOU KNOW YOUR FATHER WOULD STAY AND HELP *YOU*...HMMM... WELL, *I* WOULD...

WE'VE GOT A BLEEDER IN HERE!

D'OH!

OH, WAIT. THAT'S CHERRY SODA.

WOO-HOO!

SOON...

IS IT SERIOUS?

WELL, I'M NO DOCTOR, MRS. SIMPSON, BUT I'D SAY YOUR HUSBAND IS SUFFERING FROM AN ACUTE BURST APPENDIX!

IF YOU'RE *NOT* A DOCTOR, WHY DID YOU JUST EXAMINE MY HUSBAND?!

YOU HAVE *NO IDEA* HOW LONELY IT CAN GET IN A GIFT BOUTIQUE.

LATER...

OH, DAD, I'M SO GLAD YOUR OPERATION WENT OKAY.

DOES THIS HURT?

OW! CUT IT OUT!

KENT BROCKMAN HERE WITH THE *SECOND* LUCKY GOLDEN STRAW WINNER, *NELSON MUNTZ!*

LIVE! KRUSTY WATCH '99

IT WAS A LOT OF WORK SHAKING DOWN THESE DWEEBS AND STUFF, BUT IT FINALLY PAID OFF.

WHATEVER.

OKAY, S-SO WE'RE FRIENDS NOW, RIGHT?

NELSON MUNTZ, LOCAL BULLY

OH, MAN. ONLY TWO LEFT. MY CHANCES ARE DROPPING FASTER THAN MARTIN PRINCE IN A DODGEBALL GAME.

WELL NOW, HOW'S MY PATIENT DOING? I THOUGHT YOU'D LIKE TO SEE WHAT WE CUT OUT OF YOUR ENGORGED ABDOMINAL CAVITY.

EWWWW, NO!

COOL, MAN. LET ME HAVE IT.

AH, HEH! HEH! HEH!

THAT WOULD BE AGAINST HOSPITAL POLICY AND EVERY ETHICAL PRINCIPLE A MAN OF MY MEDICAL BACKGROUND BELIEVES IN...

...BUT OKAY, JUST THIS ONCE.

BUT *MAAAARGE*, THERE OUGHT TO BE A LAW! IF A MAN PASSES SOMETHING THROUGH HIS STOMACH AND THE WALL OF HIS LARGE INTESTINE, IT SHOULD BE HIS TO KEEP.

FINDERS KEEPERS, LOSERS WEEPERS, HOMER-SABE!

THAT'S IT. I WON'T STAY IN THIS CAR ANOTHER MINUTE WITH A SNEAKY STRAW-STEALING *THIEF*! LET ME OUT AT THE KWIK-E-MART.

HRRRRM...

I CAN'T BELIEVE YOU PICKED *GRAMPA* TO GO ON THE *KRUSTY TOUR* INSTEAD OF *ME*.

SORRY, HOMER. BESIDES, IT'S THE LEAST I CAN DO FOR GRAMPA AFTER PLAYING THAT TRICK ON HIM.

I KNEW YOU WERE TOO SHORT TO BE QUENTIN TARANTINO!

COME ON, GRAMPA, THERE'S ROOM IN THE CAR NOW.

APU, SET ME UP WITH A TRIPLE CAROB, CHOCOLATE-CHIP RIPPLE-SUNDAE FLAVORED SQUISHEE...AND DON'T BE STINGY WITH THE HOT FUDGE.

OH, I AM SORRY, MR. HOMER. WE ONLY CARRY KRUSTY BRAND CHERRY SODA NOW.

D'OH! I'LL HAVE ONE OF THOSE THEN.

I AM SORRY, MR. HOMER, BUT WE ARE ALL OUT OF KRUSTY BRAND CHERRY SODA.

THANK YOU, COME AGAIN. ♪

@#$%!

PSST! HEY, MISTER, LOOKIN' FOR A *GOOD TIME*?

FOR A GOOD TIME, DRINK KRUSTY BRAND CHERRY SODA

YEAH, RIGHT. WHAT DO YOU WANT FOR IT? THE SHIRT OFF MY BACK?

GLUG! GLUG! GLUG!

CLONG!

AAAAAH!
BURP!

I CAN'T BELIEVE IT! I MUST BE THE LUCKIEST MAN IN THE UNIVERSE. A FREE HALF-FULL BOTTLE OF LUKE-WARM CHERRY SODA AND A LITTLE STRAW TO DRINK IT WITH.

D'OH!

AND SO KRUSTY WATCH '99 COMES TO A FANTASTIC CONCLUSION AS THE *FOURTH* AND *FINAL* GOLDEN STRAW IS RECOVERED BY...WHAT'S YOUR NAME?...

I'M SURE I WAS UNDER THE SPEED LIMIT, OFFICER! BESIDES THAT'S NOT EVEN MY CAR!

AFTER THE WEATHER WITH HOUSTON SHOWERS, OUR SUN-TANNED WEATHERMAN, STAY TUNED FOR OUR EXCLUSIVE *KRUSTY TOUR COUNTDOWN!*

KRUSTY KEEPS GETTING RICHER WHILE *I* ROT IN JAIL. WELL, I'LL SETTLE HIS HASH! ONCE I'VE HACKED INTO KRUSTY'S COMPUTER, I'LL RUIN HIS TOUR, HIS REPUTATION, HIS LIFE ITSELF!

BWAH! HA! HA! HA! HAAAAAAAAAA!

ROBERT, *PLEASE!* KEEP IT DOWN, WON'T YOU?

I'M TRYING TO SOLVE THIS CROSSWORD PUZZLE!

OH...MY SINCEREST APOLOGIES, CECIL.

QUITE ALL RIGHT. WHAT'S A SIX-LETTER-WORD THAT STARTS WITH 'M' THAT MEANS *PSYCHOPATH* OR *LUNATIC?*

WELCOME TO THE KRUSTY BRAND FUN FACTORY *PRE-TOUR EXTRAVAGANZA SHOW!*

HI! I'M *TROY McCLURE*. YOU MAY REMEMBER ME FROM OTHER PRE-TOUR EXTRAVAGANZAS LIKE "AN EVENING IN AL CAPONE'S VAULT" AND "SPELUNKING THROUGH HEF'S UNDERGROUND PLAYMATE GROTTO."

AND HERE ARE OUR FIRST LUCKY WINNERS, *NELSON MUNTZ* AND HIS PAROLE OFFICER, *SNAKE*.

COOL BADGE, MAN.

DUDE, YOU WOULD *NOT* BELIEVE WHAT I HAD TO GO THROUGH TO GET IT.

NEXT UP IS *MR. BARNEY GUMBLE*. SAY BARNEY, WHO'S THIS VISION OF LOVELINESS WITH YOU?

HELLO, I AM BARNEY'S MOTHER. YOU MAY CALL ME...BARNEY'S MOTHER.

I HAVEN'T BEEN THIS EXCITED SINCE BABY SHAMU WAS BORN. AND I'M NOT EVEN THE FA--

LOOK EVERYBODY, THE DOOR IS OPENING.

AAAAAAH!

AAAAAAH!

SSSSH. THEY'RE MAKING A MOVIE....

OOOH, LOOK. *GEENA DAVIS!*

AAAAAAH!

HERE YOU CAN SEE THE DONATIONS WE'VE RECEIVED FOR KRUSTY'S HOME FOR UNWANTED PETS AND THE ACCOUNTANTS WHO GAVE THEIR LIVES TRYING TO COUNT IT ALL.

AWESOME! THIS MUST BE MY LUCKY DAY.

I DON'T KNOW, MAN. IT WASN'T TOO LUCKY FOR *THOSE* GUYS.

BWAH-HA-HA-HA!

I'VE HACKED THE KRUSTY COMPUTER! REVENGE WILL BE MINE! WHAT WORD COULD DESCRIBE MY GENIUS?!

'MADMAN' DOESN'T FIT.

I BEG YOUR PARDON? I SHOULD THINK *NOT,* BROTHER!

NO, NO! I WAS REFERRING TO THE CROSSWORD.

OH...YES, OF COURSE.

I'M KING OF THE WORLD!

NO, WAIT... I'M GONNA DIE!

HEY, WHAT'S GOING ON?

IT'S THE NORTH POLE. WE'RE COMING SANTA! BREAK OUT THE EGG NOG!

SETTLE DOWN. SETTLE DOWN. I THINK *THIS* EXPLAINS EVERYTHING.

KRUSTY BRAND
Frozen Food Division

OH, MAN. WHAT ROTTEN LUCK.

DUDE, WE'VE BEEN DITCHED BY THE CLOWN.

WE'RE LOST, AND IT'S COLD.

FROST CONTROL

RIGHT, SO WHAT WE NEED TO DO IS GET OUR PRIORITIES STRAIGHT. I THINK WE NEED TO...*EAT GRAMPA!*

I CAN'T FEEL MY TOES.

EAT ME?!? WHY?!?!

SHEESH. LOOK AROUND DAD. WE'RE IN THE SNOW. WE'RE LOST. WE'VE GOT TO EAT SOMEBODY.

FREON

I KNOW THAT, YOU IDIOT. BUT WHY ON EARTH WOULD YOU WANT TO EAT A SCRAWNY OLD MAN?

LET'S EAT FAT BOY!

HEY!

TOO BAD WE DON'T HAVE ANY APPLESAUCE, DUDE.

HEH, HEH. NOW TAKE IT EASY. TAKE IT EASY.

I BET MY DADDY TASTES LIKE CHICKEN.

THERE'S TOO MANY OF THEM! THE TIME FOR BRUTE FORCE AND RAW COURAGE IS OVER. IT'S TIME FOR *PLAN B!*

WHAT'S PLAN B, HOMER?

RUN FOR IT!

D'OH! WHAT IDIOT PUT A CLIFF IN THE MIDDLE OF A POPPY FIELD?

PROBABLY THE SAME IDIOT THAT PUT A POPPY FIELD UNDERGROUND.

I HATE TO ASK THIS, DAD, BUT ARE WE GOING TO DIE?

YOU LISTEN TO ME, BOY! I MAY NOT BE THE BEST DAD IN THE WORLD, I MAY NOT HAVE BEEN THERE EVERY TIME YOU NEEDED ME, BUT THERE'S *NO WAY* I'M GOING TO LET THESE MECHANICAL MONKEYS HURT YOU.

NOW, GET *BEHIND* ME, BOY!

WAAAH!

OOPS!

SHROOOOM!

HEY, HEY!

COWABUNGA!

THANKS FOR NOT DYING, BOY. YOUR MOTHER WOULD HAVE BEEN PRETTY UPSET!

WHOOSH!

OOOK!

EEE!

OOOK!

EEE! EEE!

KRUSTY BRAND MILITARY HEADQUARTERS

WOO-HOO!

COOL JET, KRUSTY.

YEAH, BUT THE GOVERNMENT WON'T LET ME SELL 'EM. THEY LOOK TOO MUCH LIKE THE REAL THING ON THE STREET.

I CANCELED THE LINE WHEN THEY TOLD ME TO PUT SOME STUPID DAY-GLO CAPS ON THE NOSE.

EEP EEP! OOK OOK!

WHAT'S THAT BOY? TROUBLE AT THE OLD MILL?

SIDESHOW BOB? HACKED INTO MY COMPUTERS? TRIED TO RUIN THE WHOLE TOUR?

WHY CAN'T YOU SPEAK IN COMPLETE SENTENCES?

THE END

The Day the NAGGING Stopped

WAKE UP BART, YOU'LL BE LATE FOR SCHOOL!

BART, WASH YOUR HANDS AND REMEMBER TO CLEAN YOUR ROOM AFTER YOUR FIELD TRIP TODAY!

LISA, CLEAN OUT SNOWBALL II'S LITTERBOX AND EMPTY YOUR SPIT VALVE!

HOMER, PUT ON A SHIRT!

BUT MARGE, IT'S CASUAL FRIDAY.

GREAT, MOM'S ON ANOTHER NAGGING RAMPAGE.

¡GA-HEY!¡ I TOLD YOU FIELD-TRIPPERS THE CLONING LAB WAS OFF LIMITS.

BUT WE'RE TWINS!

Frink Labs
formerly Springfield Observatory

HEY PROFESSOR, WHAT'S THIS?

AH! THAT, MY YOUNG FRIEND, IS A WORK IN PROGRESS THAT WILL CHANGE THE WORLD!

IT'S A *BEHAVIOR MODIFICATION RAY*. FROM THIS COMPUTER I CAN CHANGE THE PERSONALITY OF ANYONE AT ANY ADDRESS IN SPRINGFIELD!

DOES IT REALLY WORK?

COCKTAIL WEENIE, DUDE?

THANK YOU, MY POLITE, NON-SOCIOPATHIC FRIEND!

COOOOOL! LEMME TRY IT! WHERE'S THE *NO MORE NAGGING* SETTING?

ARE YOU INSANE? ¡GA-HOY-A-HEY!¡ WHAT KIND OF IRRESPONSIBLE MANIAC WOULD LET A DEVICE LIKE *THIS* FALL INTO THE HANDS OF A CHILD?

JUST FOR THAT YOU STAY HERE WITH THE BEHAVIOR MODIFIER WHILE THE REST OF US FINISH THE TOUR!

STORY
IAN BOOTHBY

PENCILS
JULIUS PREITE

INKS
TIM HARKINS

LETTERS
KAREN BATES

COLORS
CHRIS UNGAR

EDITOR
BILL MORRISON

NITPICKER
MATT GROENING

*YOU HAVE DIRTIED YOUR NICE PANTS WITH CHOCOLATE

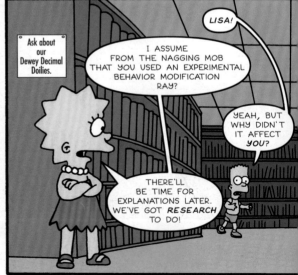

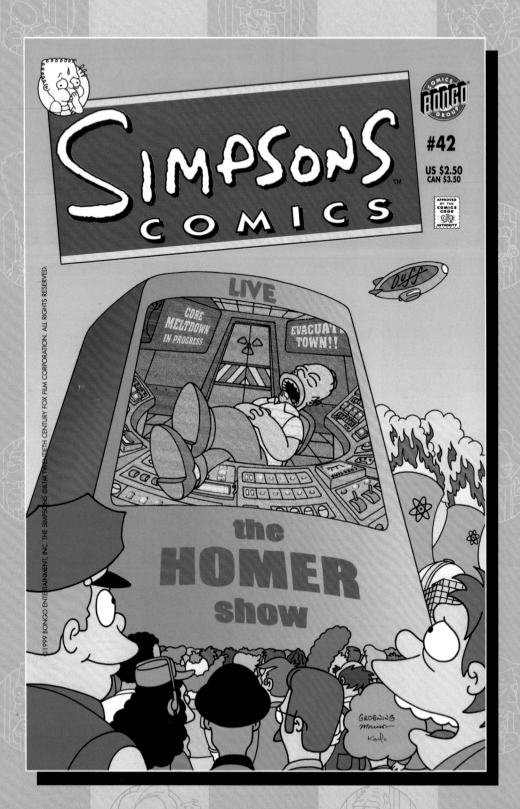

THE HOMER SHOW

THAT GUY LOOKS *FAMILIAR.*

YEAH...

SCRIPT	PENCILS	INKS	LETTERS	COLORS	MR. TELEVISION
CHUCK DIXON	PHIL ORTIZ	TIM BAVINGTON	JEANNINE BLACK	NATHAN KANE	MATT GROENING

151

ER, AH, YOU HOLLYWOOD SHARPIES HAVE TAKEN ADVANTAGE OF US BEFORE.

I SAY WE ARE NOT RUBES HERE IN SPRINGFIELD.

MAYOR QUIMBY

SPRINGFIELD

SOFT MONEY

THE CREW FROM "RADIOACTIVE MAN: THE MOVIE" GOT OUT OF TOWN WITHOUT PAYING THE CROISSANT TAX.

A BUNCH OF IMMORAL PREDATORS.

THOSE WERE *MOVIE* PEOPLE, MAYOR QUIMBY.

WE'RE IN *TELEVISION*, YOUR HONOR.

ER, A LITTLE TO THE LEFT, INGA.

ER, AH, WHAT'S THE DIFFERENCE?

WE'RE AMORAL PREDATORS, MR. MAYOR.

NO...

MOTHER OF GOD, IT *CAN'T* BE!

WE'RE SORRY TO HAVE CALLED THE ENTIRE POPULATION OF SPRINGFIELD TO THIS MEETING TONIGHT.

MAN, WHAT A TURNOUT. ARE THESE MEETINGS *USUALLY* THIS WELL ATTENDED?

WE'RE HERE 'CAUSE WE HEARD YOU GOT A BUTTLOAD OF *CASH* TO THROW AROUND.

OH.

WELL, THEN LET'S GET RIGHT TO THE POINT.

TWO HOURS LATER...

...AND SO WE'LL BE WIRING THE ENTIRE TOWN FOR VIDEO.

BUT SECRECY IS OF THE *UTMOST* IMPORTANCE. *NONE* OF THE SIMPSON FAMILY MUST KNOW THAT HOMER SIMPSON IS BEING TAPED.

AND EXACTLY *HOW* DO *WE* BENEFIT FROM THIS?

THE FOX TELEVISION NETWORK WILL PAY FOR THE CONSTRUCTION OF A COMMUNITY ARTS CENTER.

OR WE COULD JUST THROW A BUTTLOAD OF *CASH* AROUND.

LIBERTY AND JUSTICE FOR ALL

YAAAAAAAAAAY!

SPRINGFIELD COUNTY COURT HOUSE

DID YOU HEAR THAT?

HUH?

IT SOUNDED LIKE *CHEERING.*

PROBABLY THE *FLANDERSES*, MARGE. THEY'RE ALWAYS CHEERING ABOUT *GOD* OR *SIN* OR SOMETHING.

HMMMM...

HOW WAS YOUR DAY, HOMEY?

OKAY, I GUESS. EXCEPT FOR EVERY STORE DOWNTOWN BEING CLOSED FOR NO GOOD REASON.

THE SMOKE DETECTOR INSPECTORS WERE HERE.

YEAH?

THEY MADE THE KIDS AND ME LEAVE THE HOUSE FOR *HOURS* WHILE THEY CHECKED OUR BATTERIES.

THEY WERE VERY NICE ABOUT IT, BUT I HAVE A *FUNNY FEELING...*

ZZZZZZZZZ...

GOOD NIGHT, HOMER.

YEAH. GOODNIGHT, HOMER.

HOW'S OUR LATEST HIT, GENTLEMEN?

BEAUTIFUL, CHIEF.

THIS GUY'S AN ARTIST.

LET'S SEE WHAT YOU'VE GOT, BOYS.

HE CUT HIMSELF SHAVING.

D'OH!

THEN HE DID THIS TO STOP THE BLEEDING.

THIS'LL STOP IT...

THEN HE FELL DOWN THE STAIRS.

WHOAP!

AND IT'S NOT EVEN NINE IN THE MORNING?

LOOK! HE JUST STABBED HIMSELF WITH A BUTTER KNIFE!

HA HA HA!

HA

HA!

WAY TO BE, HOMER.

HA HA HA!

MAYBE HE SHOULD HAVE HIS OWN CHANNEL!

AS WEEKS GO BY, HOMER SIMPSON BECOMES A NATIONAL OBSESSION.

TV

Fox's (not so) brightest star

GOD !!!!

NEWSWEEKLY
MONTHLY

IT'S HIP TO BE A "D'OHP"!

THE NATIONAL CONSPIRER

Aliens Stole Homer's Brain-- and brought it BACK!

HOLLYWOOD INSIDER

DOOFUS IS BOFFO IN SYNDIE-INDIE DEAL.

HE SHOULD BE LEAVING THE HOUSE ANY MINUTE.

HOW MANY TIMES HAS HE RUN OVER THE MAILBOX?

THE VERMINATORS
PEST CONTROL

THE SIMPSONS

THIS WEEK? FOUR.

BAM!

THAT'S FRANKIE BACK WITH THE DONUTS.

YOU'RE NOT FRANKIE.

IT WASN'T ME! THIS ISN'T EVEN MY BALL!

WHOA-HO-HE!

YOU'RE WATCHING OUR HOUSE!

$#@&!

163

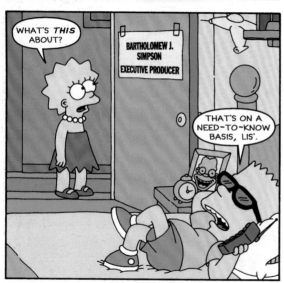

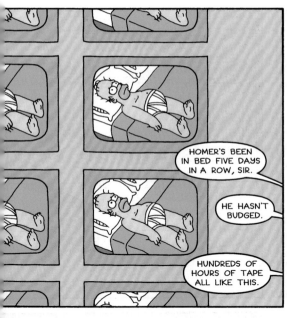

HOMER'S BEEN IN BED FIVE DAYS IN A ROW, SIR.

HE HASN'T BUDGED.

HUNDREDS OF HOURS OF TAPE ALL LIKE THIS.

OUR ENTIRE SCHEDULE RESTS ON THIS SHOW.

I HAD HOPED IT WOULDN'T COME TO THIS, BUT SOMETHING'S GOT TO BE DONE!

SOON...

AND SO I'VE COME TO APPEAL DIRECTLY TO *YOU*, MR. SIMPSON.

FOX

WITHOUT YOUR *KNOWING* IT, AMERICA HAS COME TO *LOVE* YOU.

NOT IN *SPITE* OF YOUR FAULTS BUT *BECAUSE* OF THEM. AMERICA'S NOT LAUGHING *AT* YOU, HOMER. IT'S LAUGHING *ABOUT* YOU.

THIS COUNTRY, AND THIS NETWORK, NEED YOU TO CONTINUE YOUR SENSELESS BEHAVIOR AND RECKLESS DISREGARD FOR YOUR OWN DIGNITY.

CAN YOU DO IT, HOMER? FOR YOUR MILLIONS OF FANS?

YOU CAN COUNT ON ME!

AND SO IN THE ENSUING DAYS...

OH NO! I'M WEARING A *LADIES'* HAT!

HARDWARE

OH! OH! I'VE *FALLEN* AND I *CAN'T* GET UP!

SECTOR 7G

THEN THE POLAR BEAR SAYS TO THE RABBI...

ONE MORE JOKE AND I MUST KILL YOU, MR. HOMER.

Duff BEER SALE!

OOPS!

LOOKS LIKE I FORGOT MY *PANTS* AGAIN!

WHAT'S HE DOING?

GOOD LORD, HE'S--

--*TRYING* TO BE FUNNY.

WHY DID WE EVER *LIKE* THIS SHOW?

PUT ON THE WEATHER CHANNEL!

THE NASHVILLE NETWORK!

TURN IT *OFF,* EVEN!

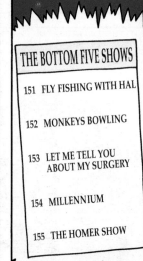

THE BOTTOM FIVE SHOWS

151 FLY FISHING WITH HAL

152 MONKEYS BOWLING

153 LET ME TELL YOU ABOUT MY SURGERY

154 MILLENNIUM

155 THE HOMER SHOW

NOT MY BIGSCREEN!

NOT MY SECRETARY!

NOT MY LATTE MACHINE!

CAN'T WE NEGOTIATE?

THANKS A *LOT*, HOMER.

YOU EVEN BUNGLED BEING A BUNGLER.

FAME ISN'T EVERYTHING, BOY.

AS THE GREAT WORDSMITH, PAT SAJAK, ONCE SAID...

"ALL GLORY IS FLEETING." NOW, INSTEAD OF SHARING MY ZANY ANTICS WITH THE WORLD, I'LL JUST SHARE THEM WITH MY FAM--

D'OH!

MMPH!

MMPH!

THE VERMINATORS PEST CONTROL

OCH!

ABC WILL PAY A *FORTUNE* FOR THIS!

THE END

SLOBBERWACKY

'Twas Wiggum, and his slimy rogues,

Did cheat to win the three-leg'd race:

All tipsy were the friends of Moe,

And Nelson stole third base.

"Beware the Slobberwack, my son! The jaws that drool, the paunch that sags!"

Beware the Jub-Jub beast, and shun...

...Jub-Jub's owners, the sister-hags!"

Bart took his trusty sling in hand:

Long time away from the games and kites—

So rested he by the Duff billboard, and grumbled loudly...

...For it was Barney Gumble.

"And, has thou slain the Slobberwack?

Come to my arms, my fearless gent!

O frabjous day! Callooh! Callay!" (Who knew what Homer meant?)

THAT'S RIGHT, JUST RELAX. NOBODY MAKES A MOVE FOR THE COCONUT CREAM.

'Twas Wiggum and his slimy rogues, Did cheat to win the pie-eating race;

All tipsy were the friends of Moe,

THE TIME HAS COME, THE WALRUS SAID, TO TALK OF MANY THINGS...

OH, MAN!

BURRRP

NOW, THIS IS THE WAY IT OUGHTA BE.

OF CABBAGES AND KINGS!

WHERE DO YOU THINK YOU'RE GOING, BOY?

MOMMY, THE SMELLY MEN ARE BEING FUNNY AGAIN!

And Flanders tried to say grace.

THE END

STORY — JESSE LEON McCANN   PENCILS — JAMES LLOYD   INKS — TIM BAVINGTON   LETTERS — KAREN BATES   COLORS — NATHAN KANE   EDITS — BILL MORRISON   JABBERWOCKY — MATT GROENING